PAUL MARTIN is an award-winning, world-record-holding cocktail mixologist, trainer and motivational speaker. Throughout his bartending career he set two world speed-cocktail-mixing records and won seven global mixology titles. He runs some of the most sought-after bartender and hospitality training courses and has trained more than 30,000 bartenders in more than 25 countries around the world. Paul has appeared in his role of 'cocktail expert' on TV and radio on many occasions including for three full series on Food Network Daily in the 1990s. Paul is also an accomplished motivational speaker and can often be found delivering talks on human connection, communication skills and other human interaction topics.

101 Award-Winning

COCKTAILS

from the World's Best Bartenders

PAUL MARTIN

ROBINSON

ROBINSON

First published in Great Britain in 2018 by Robinson

Copyright © Paul Martin, 2018

For photo credits, see page 212

3 5 7 9 10 8 6 4 2

A CIP catalogue record for this book is available
from the British Library.

ISBN 978-1-47214-053-1

Design & typography by Andrew Barron,
Thextension

Printed in the United Kingdom by Ashford Colour Press Ltd

Papers used by Robinson are from well-managed forests
and other responsible sources.

Robinson
An imprint of
Little, Brown Book Group
Carmelite House
50 Victoria Embankment
London EC4Y 0DZ

An Hachette UK Company
www.hachette.co.uk

www.littlebrown.co.uk

This book is dedicated to my beautiful wife Sheryl. Her endless love and support is a constant inspiration to me, and without which I would never have achieved the enormous challenge of compiling this book.

CONTENTS

INTRODUCTION
PAUL MARTIN

WELCOME TO *101 Award-Winning Cocktails*, probably the greatest collection of cocktail recipes ever assembled.

For the first time ever, through this book, I am giving the reader a glimpse into the world of the competition mixologist. The recipes that you'll find within these pages are the endeavours of the world's greatest living cocktail makers. These are the recipes that you've never heard of but which deliver the most wonderful drinking experiences. They won't be found in your average cocktail book or on your high-street cocktail menu. They are the cocktails that the global bartender community revere and yet only a handful of people ever get to hear about, let alone have the opportunity to try. And why? Because these cocktails are created for entry into the world's most competitive cocktail competitions, where the finest mixing talent competes for glory and peer recognition in an attempt to stun the world with their ever-evolving imagination and creativity. These are the drinks that define the drinking trends, the way you drink today, acting as motivation and influence to the millions of bartenders working the world's bars but rarely ending up in the glasses of patrons. Think of these drinks as you would a concept car or a fashion designer's catwalk show content.

Here you won't find recipes for Espresso Martinis, Mojitos or Cosmopolitans; you can find those in every other recipe book out there (and on pretty much every cocktail menu you're likely to choose a drink from). Instead, what you have is access to the drinks that have won the world's biggest competitions, sometimes beating many thousands of other fabulous cocktails to achieve ultimate glory. These are the drinks that are considered the finest inventions in their country, continent or even planet!

And why are they the best recipes ever? Because of the skills, pedigree and experience of their amazing creators. These recipes are a result of skill and creativity of the very highest level. They demonstrate the ability to identify and combine ingredients with a genius touch, ultimately resulting in taste sensations rarely experienced.

For each of our amazing 101 award-winning cocktails, we'll also introduce you to the bartender responsible for its creation. You'll discover their background, awards, achievements and career path. You'll hear direct from them too, discovering what motivated them to create the drinks we have included and with which they went on to win one of the world's great competitions. And finally, you'll have access to their recipes, the recipes that for all previous generations – outside of the mixologist community plus a few customers that may have walked into the winning bartender's place of work – simply remained out of reach.

From my point of view, as a mixologist and author of more than 30 years' experience, I compiled this book using the following criteria: Firstly, I approached the people that I consider to be the most influential bartenders of our time, most of whom I have known for longer than I care to think about. These mixologists are absolute giants of the cocktail world and are known universally for the contribution and impact they have made to the global bartending scene. Next, I offered award-winning bartenders the world over the opportunity to submit their recipes for inclusion with a single criterion – their cocktail had to have won a major cocktail competition. In all I received more than 500 additional submissions from which I selected around 50 based on just how delicious they are. In fact, on one or two occasions I have even selected cocktails that didn't win their competition (maybe, coming second: silver still being an award-winner) but in my opinion were such fantastic recipes that I just had to share them with you! In my view, the cocktails included within these pages are without doubt the greatest drinks around.

So, if you want to truly stun your guests next time you dig a shaker out, forget the usual stuff and give them a taste sensation that will not only blow their minds but is officially recognised as one of the most inspired alcoholic concoctions on the planet.

A PEAR(IS) ROMANCE
BC HOFFMAN

BC says: *This is the cocktail that had me win the Marie Brizard competition in 2016 for all of Southern California. It was just approaching fall, and I really wanted to bring an element that reminded me of living back in colder temperatures during this time of year and going to pick fresh pears with my family, and then get a hot spiced cider afterwards.*

15ML MARIE BRIZARD PEAR WILLIAM
15ML DRY VERMOUTH
45ML JAMESON IRISH WHISKEY
15ML SPICED MAPLE SYRUP*
15ML FRESH LEMON JUICE
15ML FRESH PEAR JUICE
POIRE AUTHENTIQUE PEAR CIDER, TO TOP UP

METHOD: Add all the ingredients to a shaker with a scoop of ice and shake well. Strain into an ice-filled Collins glass and top with pear cider.

SPICED MAPLE SYRUP*
Add 2 cinnamon sticks, 5 cardamom pods, 3 whole cloves and 2 tsp whole black peppercorns to a sauté pan and lightly toast. Add 475ml maple syrup and 1 vanilla pod, sliced in half (if unavailable use 1 tsp vanilla extract), and heat for 5–10 minutes. Remove from the heat and leave to cool for 1 hour with the spices still in the syrup. Strain the syrup and bottle.

———————

BC HOFFMAN is a truly multi-talented hospitality professional whose expertise lies well beyond mixology alone. As the owner of Chef BC at DC Catering, he provides consultancy to the hospitality industry on topics ranging from cocktails to sushi. His career to date spans more than 15 years, during which time he has held a range of diverse positions from executive chef at Posh in Washington DC, through to head bartender at Old Fields Liquor Room in Venice, California. As a mixologist, he has drawn on his culinary skills to consistently create complex and inventive cocktail recipes. Many of these have gone on to win competitions and awards including the Global Mandarine Napoleon Cocktail Competition in 2013, the Amaro Montenegro Cocktail Competition in 2016, the Ketel One Competition in 2016 (later demonstrated live on *Jimmy Kimmel Live!*) and the regional Mionetto Competition in New York, also in 2016.

WINNER OF THE MARIE BRIZARD COCKTAIL COMPETITION 2016

ADMIRAL'S SALUTE
DARREN MILEY

Darren says: *A salute is a gesture of respect or polite recognition, especially one made to or by a person when arriving or departing. Every day, everywhere on this planet, there are people whose amazing achievements go unnoticed. This cocktail is my tribute to them all, so they in turn can raise a glass in salute of those in their world who deserve celebration.*

45ML BACARDI OCHO RUM
20ML COCCHI AMERICANO
10ML TIO PEPE FINO SHERRY
7.5ML GRENADINE
1 DASH FEE BROTHERS PEACH BITTERS
1 DASH ANGOSTURA BITTERS

METHOD: Add all the ingredients to the shaker with a scoop of ice. Shake well, then double strain into a coupette glass. Garnish with twisted orange peel.

————

DARREN MILEY is an Irish bartender who lives and works in Auckland, New Zealand. Having gained his formal education in Ireland, including an honours degree in mechanical engineering, Darren embarked on his travels, a journey that would lead him to New Zealand and the commencement of a career (to date) in bartending. Since 2012, Darren has worked his way up the mixology ladder, starting in the role of bartender and rising to his current position of Beverage Innovation and Training Manager. Whilst Darren may not have competed in as many competitions as some of our award-winning bartenders, the two that he has done clearly reflect a natural ability for developing creative cocktail mixes. In 2016 he managed a highly impressive third place in the revered 42Below Cocktail Earth Cup, then followed that up with his win in the Bacardi Legacy Competition 2017, with his New Zealand victory leading to a creditable eighth place in the global championships.

WINNER OF BACARDI LEGACY NEW ZEALAND 2017

AEGIRS FIZZ

ADAM SPINKS

Adam Says: *I wanted to pay tribute to Icelandic heritage and also to combine a mixture of ingredients from the ancient Scandinavian gods of Norse mythology. Firstly Sol, the God of the sun, picked up in the Solerno-infused marmalade. The bladderwrack seaweed represents Aegir, the god of the sea. Applewood is a tribute to Yggdrasil, the ash tree that connects the nine worlds together in Norse mythology. Finally, Vidar, the god of the forest, is represented by the use of Icelandic moss.*

50ML REYKA VODKA
2 BSP SOLERNO-INFUSED MARMALADE WITH VOLCANIC MOSS*
10ML APPLEWOOD-SMOKED BLADDERWRACK SEAWEED SYRUP**
1 EGG WHITE
12.5ML FRESH LEMON JUICE
2 DASHES REYKA BITTERS
1724 TONIC, TO TOP UP

METHOD: Shake all the ingredients with ice and serve in a pewter tankard straight up. Top with 1724 tonic and add 2 bay leaves to garnish.

SOLERNO-INFUSED MARMALADE WITH VOLCANIC MOSS* My family secret marmalade that was soaked in Icelandic volcanic moss and Solerno blood orange liqueur for 6 hours.

APPLEWOOD-SMOKED BLADDERWRACK SEAWEED SYRUP** Smoke 20g dried bladderwrack seaweed with applewood for 17 hours on rotation. Boil with 70ml water adding 4 tbsp demerara sugar, then leave to cool.

———————

ADAM SPINKS is a rising star who has been bartending for more than 10 years. At the time of writing he is the general manager of the Kilburn Ironworks in London. This is the latest in a run of high-profile appointments, including the five-star Belgravia Hotel, that underlines the esteem in which he is held. In fact, Adam's knowledge and skills in regard to cocktails and mixology also mean that he not only competes (and wins) cocktail competitions, but also regularly features on competition judging panels too. Adam's knowledge of spirits and liqueurs is extensive, especially concerning gin (he describes himself as a 'gin enthusiast'). In addition, his love for the history of his trade not only supplies inspiration and influence for his cocktail creations but also provides the basis for another of his passions: collecting antique barware and glasses. On the competition front, his creative skills have seen him reach the final of countless competitions including the Disaronno Mixing Star, the Sloane Gin Cocktail Competition and the Flor de Caña Cocktail Competition.

WINNER OF REYKA WORLD'S FIRST 24-HOUR COCKTAIL COMPETITION 2015

ALCO BRUNCH
POCHOLO DOBANDIDS

Pocholo says: *The drink's inspiration would be my quest to have a taste-shifting drink that depends on the preference of the drinker. Flavour is subjective, so I figured I would create a drink in which one flavour is dominant, but once you bite onto the chocolate cup the subtle notes come through replacing the initial ginger spicy notes that you will first taste. It's all up to the guests.*

60ML TALISKER 10 WHISKY

20ML ORANGE MARMALADE

15ML GINGER SHRUB

30ML RAMAZZOTTI

1 EGG

3 DASHES CHOCOLATE BITTERS

A CHOCOLATE CUP*, TO SERVE

METHOD: Add all the ingredients to a shaker and dry shake. Add a scoop of ice and shake again. Strain into a chocolate cup and garnish with chopped candied ginger.

Using a ball-shaped mould*, create the cup using 70 per cent dark chocolate.

————

POCHOLO DOBANDIDS has been bartending since 2013, including a period as principal bartender at The Curator Coffee & Cocktails Inc, during which time it was rated in Asia's top 50 bars. Currently the bar supervisor at the Shangri-La at the Fort, Manila, Pocholo is also responsible for the training of all the hotel's up and coming bartenders. In 2014, Pocholo was included in Gary Regan's book, *101 Best New Cocktails*, and also came runner-up in the Cointreau Cocktail competition. His 2015 win in the Monkey Shoulder Ultimate Bartender Championship was followed by another runner-up spot in the 2016 Whisky Live competition.

WINNER OF MONKEY SHOULDER ULTIMATE BARTENDER CHAMPIONSHIP 2015

AMERITINO
MANOLIS LYKIARDOPOULOS

Manolis says: *The inspiration for my cocktail is the history of vermouth and the trends behind the bar these days. Ameritino is a new modern aperitivo cocktail based on the classic Italian vermouth cocktails. I have enhanced modern elements and added some traditional Greek ingredients.*

50ML MARTINI RISERVA SPECIALE RUBINO
15ML MARTINI
10ML SKINOS MASTIHA SPIRIT
8ML ESPRESSO COFFEE
50ML THREE CENTS TONIC WATER

METHOD: Add all the ingredients but the tonic to a mixing glass with a scoop of ice and stir for 10 seconds. Strain into an ice-filled highball glass, add the tonic and stir gently. Garnish with lemon peel and fresh marjoram leaves.

MANOLIS LYKIARDOPOULOS is widely known across the bartending world due in large part to his amazing success in global competitions over recent years. In addition to winning the highly prestigious Martini Grand Prix, he won the Greek Disaronno Mixing Star competition in 2014, became Diageo World Class Greece champion in 2015 and went on to place fifth in the world at the global finals in South Africa the same year. Manolis has a particular passion for vermouth and has consequently opened and co-owns the Odori Vermuteria di Atene, the first ever vermouth bar in Greece.

WINNER OF MARTINI GRAND PRIX 2016

AN ENDLESS JOURNEY
GREG ALMEIDA

Greg says: *My cocktail is all about the journey of life and what you make of it. When you meet people, you become inspired and it's what you do with those inspirations that can change your life. I wanted my cocktail to inspire my guests and for them to make it a part of their journey. Patrón tequila represents tradition at its core and innovation in its approach, and to me, that is inspirational.*

35ML PATRÓN REPOSADO TEQUILA
10ML MEXICAN MOLE BITTERS
5ML SUZE
2 DASHES VANILLA BITTERS
60ML JASMINE AND ALMOND HORCHATA*

METHOD: Place all the ingredients in a mixing glass with ice, and do the 'Cuban Roll' (pouring the contents back and forth between mixing glass and shaker tin). Strain into a chilled wooden cup with no ice. Garnish with grated nutmeg.

JASMINE AND ALMOND HORCHATA*
Add 100g white long-grain rice to a blender with 700ml water and 40g whole blanched almonds and blend for 1 minute. Pour into a container and allow to stand for 3 hours. Next, strain the liquid into a bowl and stir in 80ml milk, 100g caster sugar, 1 tsp vanilla extract, 2 tsp ground cinnamon and 1 tsp jasmine essence. Chill until required.

GREG ALMEIDA started his bartending career in 2008 in France at the 5-star Royal Riviera Hotel and by 2009 had become their head bartender. By 2010 he had moved to Canada and was working at the LAB, Comptoir à Cocktails cocktail bar, where he once again became the bar manager within a year. His move to London came in 2012 where he first worked at the Novikov Lounge and then moved on to the Michelin-starred Pollen Street Social, where he yet again reached the role of head bartender. There is no doubting Greg's skills as a mixologist. Prior to becoming the Patrón Perfectionist national champion, he had achieved second place at the Montreal Bar Chef competition in 2011, and had reached the UK finals of four other respected UK competitions.

WINNER OF PATRÓN PERFECTIONIST UK NATIONAL FINALS 2017

APOSTOL
GRACE TSAI

Grace says: *Apostol is about a people who have a strong faith and believe in it deeply. It's for everyone who has looked for their passion, purpose or faith – a thing in our life that makes us feel whole. Apostol is more than a cocktail; it's a true story about passionate people who champion their beliefs despite any hardship. I hope everyone can be an Apostol of our faith, be the legend of our life, and let's keep passing down our own legacy.*

40ML BACARDI OCHO RUM
15ML MITCHER'S RYE WHISKEY
15ML CUESTA P.X. SHERRY
10ML MOZART DARK CHOCOLATE LIQUEUR

METHOD: Add all the ingredients to a mixing glass with a scoop of ice and stir well. Strain into a brandy snifter. Garnish with a piece of orange peel and serve beside flamed cinnamon powder*.

FLAMED CINNAMON POWDER*
Grind a cinnamon stick into small pieces and place in a pile beside the drink. Using a kitchen blowtorch (or other naked flame), burn the pile until it begins to smoulder. Extinguish the flame, leaving the pile to 'smoke'.

GRACE TSAI is possibly the least experienced bartender to appear in this book – a fact that makes her award-winning cocktail even more impressive. Unlike the other award-winning bartenders, this is Grace's only competition. Coming from Taiwan, Grace entered the bartending profession without family support. In her own words, she explains that 'all of my family disagree with my choice of being a bartender, especially as I was a girl and the only child to my mom'. At the time she was unsure of whether she had made the correct choice but decided to enter the Bacardi Legacy Competition as an opportunity to gain greater experience and to decide whether to walk away. The result was an incredible win for Grace, and totally unexpected exposure to the potential career and opportunities available to top-class professional mixologists.

WINNER OF BACARDI LEGACY TAIWAN 2016

BAYTOUTY

KEVIN HADDAD

Kevin says: *My cocktail was inspired by a small shop that sells homemade local products located in the cedar forests of Mount Lebanon. This shop is really famous for its carob molasses and they used to serve a Lebanese traditional dessert made from carob molasses and tahini to all their clients. I wanted to create a cocktail with the same character.*

5ML RON ZACAPA 23 RUM
5 DROPS ARAK
5ML TAHINI TINCTURE
20ML THYME-INFUSED CAROB MOLASSES*

METHOD: Add all the ingredients to a cocktail shaker with a scoop of ice and shake hard for 10 seconds. Strain into an ice-filled tumbler and garnish with orange slices.

THYME-INFUSED CAROB MOLASSES*
Add 3 sprigs of thyme to 200ml carob molasses and allow to infuse for 1 week.

————————

KEVIN HADDAD commenced his bartending career in 2009 working as a bar-back and trainee in a bar in Antelias. Thereafter, Kevin has worked in, and co-owned, a number of bars resulting in his last head bartender role at the Italian Project in Mar Mikhaël, Beirut. Since Kevin's Diageo World Class success, he has worked as a brand ambassador for Diageo. In April 2015, Kevin became the Lebanese champion at the Skinos Cocktail championships and then went on to represent his country in the global finals in Greece, where he finished as runner-up.

BIG FISH
VITALY ALEKSEYEV

Vitaly says: *Every drinking experience starts with a story, it's what makes people thirsty and use their imagination. The name comes from the tall tales of fisherman and the 'big fish' that got away. Bartenders around the world are the modern-day storytellers, authors and poets. All of the ingredients I use are paying tribute to the origins of Bacardi Ocho and to the author's family. A good drink is like a good story: it is meant to be enjoyed over and over again.*

50ML BACARDI OCHO RUM
20ML EARL GREY SYRUP*
10ML TIO PEPE FINO SHERRY
2.5ML SHERRY VINEGAR

METHOD: Add all the ingredients to a mixing glass with a scoop of ice and stir. Strain into an ice-filled old-fashioned glass and garnish with a bay leaf and a maraschino cherry on a cocktail stick (optional).

EARL GREY SYRUP*
Make 500ml of Earl Grey tea. Add 300g sugar and stir over a low heat until the sugar has completely dissolved. Allow to cool, then store in a sealed bottle.

———————

VITALY ALEKSEYEV's first job was at the Hilton Hotel on London's Park Lane in 2013. Within 10 months, Vitaly had moved on to open the brand-new Cocktail Embassy in south-east London, where he also became the head bartender. After 18 months of creating new menus, training staff and running cocktail masterclasses for the customers, Vitaly moved to Amsterdam to work for the Entourage Group, one of the biggest hospitality companies in the Netherlands. Vitaly's impact on the team at the Duchess Bar resulted in them winning the award for Netherland's Best Cocktail Bar 2016 and served as a forerunner to his personal success in becoming the national champion for the Netherlands at Bacardi Legacy 2017.

BLUE-CUMBER
BRIAN VAN FLANDERN

Brian says: *While I personally avoid flavoured vodkas, Stolichnaya Blueberry was one of the sponsors. I used it sparingly while staying true to the flavour profile. The recipe was completely impromptu and was created on-the-fly when the secret ingredient of cucumbers was revealed. The result was a very light and refreshing summertime drink that surprised even me.*

35ML BARSOL MOSTO VERDE PISCO
7ML STOLICHNAYA BLUEBERRY VODKA
28ML WHOLE ENGLISH CUCUMBER JUICE*
14ML FRESH LIME JUICE
28ML SIMPLE SYRUP
28ML MOSCATO D'ASTI SPARKLING WINE

METHOD: Place all the ingredients (except the sparkling wine) into a shaker, add a large amount of ice and shake vigorously. Open the shaker, add the Moscato wine, close the shaker again and then tumble (roll back and forth) one time. Double strain into a highball glass over fresh ice and garnish with a cucumber ribbon skewered with alternating blueberries.

WHOLE ENGLISH CUCUMBER JUICE*
Take 1 whole English cucumber and chop into pieces (keep the skin on). Blend the cucumber until smooth, then strain it through a muslin cloth to remove the solids. Refrigerate.

———————

BRIAN VAN FLANDERN is a world-renowned mixologist and author who has worked in New York for over 25 years and has been named America's Top Mixologist by the Food Network. In 2006 Brian founded Creative Cocktail Consultants, a global beverage consulting firm dedicated to spirits education, innovating cutting-edge cocktail lists, and training professional bartenders in the art of mixology. He has appeared on American TV on numerous occasions, including appearances on CBS's *The Early Show*. In 2004 he opened the three Michelin-star restaurant Per Se and in 2006 was ranked as the number two bartender in the world. Two thousand and nine saw the release of his best-selling book, *Vintage Cocktails*, named Best Cocktail Book in the World by the Gourmand Cookbook Awards in Paris. Brian is also the author of *Craft Cocktails*, *Celebrity Cocktails* and *Tequila Cocktails*, which is a collaboration with movie star George Clooney.

WINNER OF UNITED STATES BARTENDERS' GUILD IRON BAR CHEF COMPETITION 2007

BLUSHING MONARCH
SALIM KHOURY

Salim says: *My unique cocktail, created in the early 90s when I was working at The Savoy, was called 'Blushing Monarch' and won me the coveted title of Barman of the Year. It was the overwhelming winner with the judges. My inspiration in those days was Princess Diana, and when one of the judges asked me why I called it that, my answer was, 'It was pink, it was elegant, it was blushing!'*

40ML CAMPARI
20ML GIN
20ML COINTREAU
15ML PASSION FRUIT JUICE
1 EGG WHITE (OPTIONAL)

METHOD: Add all the ingredients to a shaker with a scoop of ice and shake well. Strain into an ice-filled highball glass or other tall glass and garnish with half a passion fruit (optional).

———————

SALIM KHOURY is one of my favourite people from the world of bartending. Born in Lebanon, he began his bartending career in 1960 as a 15-year-old, working behind the bar at the Bristol Hotel in Beirut. Nine years later, he arrived in the UK and took a job at the iconic American Bar at the Savoy Hotel in London. Salim stayed in that job for his entire career, until 2012 when he took a well-earned retirement. In those 42 years, Salim rose to become the American Bar's head bartender and in the course of events also became a bartending legend. Salim is known and respected right across the global bartending community and is one of the most recognisable faces from the world of cocktails... period! In 1993 Salim won the coveted Bartender of the Year title (at a time when competitions like Diageo World Class and Bacardi Legacy didn't exist), an achievement he cites as the proudest of his career. Likewise, I am proud to include it in this book.
Note: Enjoy the golf Salim. P

WINNER OF BARTENDER OF THE YEAR 1993

BOLD PILOT
ENGIN YILDIZ

Engin says: *This exciting cocktail was inspired by a farmer. He was a busy farmer, growing grains, importing almonds, running bee hives and making blackberry jam. One day a customer entered his shop holding a valuable bottle of blended whisky and bought a bottle of Talisker as a gift. At the customer's request, the farmer combined both whiskies with a variety of farm produce, allowing them to steep in a jar. When they tried the mixture, they decided to name it after the farmer's horse, Bold Pilot.*

45ML JOHNNIE WALKER BLUE LABEL WHISKY
15ML TALISKER TEN WHISKY
45ML FRESH PEAR JUICE
2 BSP BLACKBERRY JAM
2 DASHES ALMOND AND HONEY BITTERS*

METHOD: Combine all of the ingredients in a mixing glass with a scoop of ice. Stir for 10 seconds, then strain into an ice-filled vintage rocks glass. Garnish with grated almond and pear peels infused with sage tea.

ALMOND AND HONEY BITTERS*
Add the following ingredients to 1 litre ethyl alcohol: 10 star anise, 5 cinnamon sticks, 1 tbsp cloves, 1 tsp dried sage tea, peel from 1 orange and 2 lemons, 1 vanilla pod, 200ml orgeat syrup, 1 tbsp dried red apple tea and 50g crushed roasted almonds. Keep in an airtight container for 17 days in a dark area at room temperature.

In a separate airtight container combine 75g quality Turkish honeycomb honey with 250ml ethyl alcohol and 250ml water. Likewise keep for 17 days, stirring daily.

After 17 days combine the two containers and keep for an additional 10 days, stirring daily.

At the end of 27 days filter the contents through a fine muslin cloth or coffee filter 3–5 times, then bottle.

———

ENGIN YILDIZ is a Turkish bartender who now works in Ohio, USA. During his 16-year career he has worked across Turkey's major cities and hotspots, plying his skills behind some of the most famous bars, including Zuma in Istanbul and Blue Marlin Ibiza in Bodrum. On the competition front, Engin has climbed the ladder steadily, moving from a sixth place in 2014 to his eventual victory in 2016, which resulted in him being invited to become the brand ambassador for Ketel One vodka. Since then Elgin has become a Diageo World Class judge and made the move to the USA, where he hopes to expand his skills and experience further.

WINNER OF DIAGEO WORLD CLASS TURKEY 2016

BON VOYAGE
VALENTINO LONGO

Valentino says: *My cocktail is a tribute to Masataka Taketsuru, the founder of the Nikka whisky distillery. In 1902 he travelled from Japan to Scotland to learn how to make Scottish whisky. After training in several whisky distilleries and attending Glasgow University, he returned to Japan and set up the first ever whisky distillery there. I took my inspiration from him, his trip and dedication. Hence the name 'Bon Voyage' as it's a cocktail that you can carry on a long trip.*

50ML YOICHI 15 WHISKY
20ML COCCHI TORINO INFUSED WITH BAMBOO LEAVES*
10ML UMESHU PLUM SAKE
3 DASHES GRAPEFRUIT BITTERS

METHOD: Add all the ingredients to mixing glass without ice and stir. Strain into a whisky flask. When ready to serve, pour into an ice-filled old-fashioned glass.

COCCHI TORINO INFUSED WITH BAMBOO LEAVES*
Add 4 bamboo leaves to a bottle of Cocchi Torino vermouth and allow to stand for 24 hours. Strain out the leaves and keep the infused vermouth chilled.

VALENTINO LONGO began his career in 2011, working in his home country of Italy at the 5-star Hotel de Russie. He then moved to the UK, working as head bartender at the 5-star Corinthia Hotel before heading to one of London's greatest landmarks, the Ritz, where he tended bar for another year. During his UK tenure, Valentino reached the top three at Diageo World Class, UK and won the UK Tequila Cocktail Competition. His win at the Italian Nikka Cocktail Competition saw him represent Italy at the European finals where he placed third overall. Valentino is currently the head bartender at Four Season's Surf Club in Miami Beach.

WINNER OF THE NIKKA COCKTAIL COMPETITION ITALY 2016

BOOT UP OR BOOTLEG
ANTHONY COOK

Anthony says: *The competition brief was to give thanks through our drink. My thanks was for American football. I discovered that 1920 was the same year that both Prohibition hit America and the NFL was formed. My theory is that many of the out-of-work distillery workers were snapped up by one of the 20 new football teams. So, unlike most bartenders, I do give a little thanks to Prohibition as it was possibly the catalyst for American football. The name comes from the idea that people had the choice to boot up or bootleg!*

35ML JIM BEAM WHITE WHISKEY
25ML FRESH LEMON JUICE
50ML SALTED CARAMEL, APPLE AND GREEN TEA INFUSION*
50ML GINGER BEER
3 STRAWBERRIES, FINELY CHOPPED

METHOD: Add all the ingredients to a shaker with a scoop of ice and shake well. Strain over fresh ice in a crystal cut vintage rocks glass (use modern rocks style glass if not available) and garnish with 2 slices of caramel apple** and a mint sprig.

SALTED CARAMEL, APPLE AND
GREEN TEA INFUSION*
Add 3 salted caramel green tea bags to 330ml water, 175g caster sugar and 100ml pressed apple juice. Heat gently and stir until the sugar has dissolved and the tea fully infused. Allow to cool, then store in the fridge in a sealed container.

CARAMEL APPLES**
Caramelise the apple slices in a pan with a mixture of 2 tbsp brown sugar and 50ml Tiki Fire rum.

ANTHONY COOK is a highly experienced bar development coach. He works on creating bespoke cocktails, menus and training sessions for bars and bartenders across the UK. His current role with the Chiquito chain sees him responsible for the development of the cocktail lists and cocktail development for over 400 bartenders across 90 restaurants. With more than 15 years' experience of working with many of the UK's most recognisable restaurant brands, Anthony has developed his mixology skills to the point where his creative talents have resulted in his award-winning inclusion in this book.

CARGO
ADAM LAHHAM

Adam says: My inspiration comes from every person sitting in front of me at the bar. When we opened Scarfes Bar in Rosewood London, we had up to 280 types of whiskies. Bowmore is close to my heart and consequently, I chose it as the base spirit for my cocktail. Bowmore Whisky was hidden during the Second World War in boats in nearby Loch Indaal to prevent potential loss. The name Cargo was the first that came to my mind, representing the precious cargo.

45ML BOWMORE 15-YEAR DARKEST WHISKY
15ML AMERICANO COCCHI
½ TBSP YUZU JUICE
2–3 PINCHES GROUND BLACK PEPPER
20ML CHERRY VINEGAR-BASED PINEAPPLE SHRUB*

METHOD: Add all the ingredients to a shaker with a scoop of ice and shake well. Double strain into a crystal glass over hand-chopped ice. Garnish with a dehydrated pineapple slice and fresh Maraschino cherry (optional).

CHERRY VINEGAR-BASED PINEAPPLE SHRUB*
Heat 200ml cherry vinegar with 100g pineapple chunks and 150g sugar in a pan. Simmer for 10 minutes, then strain and allow the liquid to cool.

———————

ADAM LAHHAM is one of the cocktail world's more accomplished bartenders. Currently working in Vancouver, Canada, he tends bar at Rosewood Hotel's Reflections Bar, having previously worked at the Rosewood's London flagship. It was while based in London that Adam won the 2014 Galvin Cup. Adam has won or placed in numerous highly regarded competitions, including winning the Bloody Mary Competition at the 2010 Boutique Bar Show. His skills have also had him in demand outside of his regular hotel work, including being asked to provide the 'cocktail treatment' (run a cocktail bar) for the Duke and Duchess of Northumberland at Alnwick Castle. Adam has written for magazines and periodicals, in particular on his favourite subject of whisky. In fact, prior to his cocktail bartending career starting in 2006, his work as a whisky writer/traveller meant that he became the first Slovakian to tour the distilleries of Ardbeg, Lagavulin, Laphroaig, Bunnahabhain, Bruichladdich and Auchentoshan, a fact that he is most proud of.

WINNER OF THE GALVIN CUP 2014

CARIBBEAN JULEP
JULIEN ESCOT

Julien says: *In Cuba your senses are seriously stimulated. The heat, the flavours, the smells, the colours and sounds are all around you. So, I decided to compete with a cocktail that would be a sensorial explosion. The Julep base allowed me to play with the mint, which is a symbolic ingredient in Cuban drinking. It allowed me also to pour a double measure of Havana Club and to work on a homemade concentrate and very flavoured velvet falernum. I wanted to offer the jury Cuba in a glass!*

20ML HOMEMADE VELVET FALERNUM*
10–12 FRESH MINT LEAVES
80ML HAVANA CLUB 7-YEAR-OLD RUM
5ML THE BITTER TRUTH PIMENTO DRAM

METHOD: Into a Julep mug (or appropriate glass) add the Velvet Falernum and the mint leaves. Gently muddle to allow the mint oils to infuse. Now half fill with crushed ice, add the Havana Club and the Pimento Dram and churn with a spoon. Now top up with more crushed ice and stir once more. Garnish with mint leaves, candied orange zest and crushed spices.

HOMEMADE VELVET FALERNUM*
Into a pan, add 400ml water and 400g sugar. Warm (not boil) until the sugar has completely dissolved. Now add 2 vanilla pods, 1 stalk of lemon grass, a 1cm-cubed piece of fresh ginger, 5 cloves, 10 coffee beans and 1 tbsp ground almonds. Warm for 10–15 minutes allowing the flavours to infuse. Strain the liquid, allow to cool, then mix with 200ml Havana Club 3-year-old. Store in a screw-top container or bottle and keep refrigerated.

JULIEN ESCOT has been bartending since 1999, which makes him one of the more experienced mixologists to appear in this book. He has a reputation for being one of France's finest and as such was named as the country's Most Influential Bartender in 2013. Julien is the owner of Papa Doble in Montpellier, named as one of the 50 Best Bars in the World in 2011. Julien has also written four cocktail and mixology books, *Art Cocktail* in 2006, *Cocktails – Leçons de Dégustation* in 2012, *Alcools Cultissimes* in 2013 and *Cocktail Now* in 2015. In addition to winning the global Havana Club competition, he was also the global winner of the Drinks International Bartender Challenge in 2004.

WINNER OF HAVANA CLUB GRAND PRIX GLOBAL 2012 (WORLD CHAMPION)

THE CARIBBEAN OASIS
CALEB REEVES

Caleb says: *My goal with this cocktail was to incorporate four levels of taste: sour, sweet, spice and savoury. By doing this, I turned a classic concept like a Margarita into so much more of a beverage experience.*

3 ENGLISH CUCUMBER SLICES
1 ORANGE SLICE
20ML REHYDRATED CARIBBEAN-JERK-INFUSED BLACKBERRY PURÉE*
45ML CASAMIGOS BLANCO TEQUILA
15ML COINTREAU
20ML FRESH LIME JUICE

METHOD: Muddle the cucumber, orange and blackberry purée in a shaker. Add all the remaining ingredients with a scoop of ice and shake hard for 10 seconds. Fine strain into a chilled custom-made Alabama white alabaster stone rocks glass (you can use a regular rocks glass too) and garnish with a notched cucumber and lime slice.

REHYDRATED CARIBBEAN-JERK-INFUSED BLACKBERRY PURÉE*
Add 1 tbsp Caribbean jerk seasoning to 1 tbsp olive oil. Let it sit for 4 hours, then strain off the remaining oil. Add the seasoning into a blender with 3 handfuls of blackberries, 250ml simple syrup and 250ml hot water. Blend, then add the mixture to a pan and simmer for 5 minutes. Allow to cool, then finely strain.

CALEB REEVES began bartending in 2008 at the Auburn University Hotel and Conference Centre, where he developed the cocktail menu in 2011 and won the silver medal from the Alabama Hotel and Restaurant Alliance in 2011 and 2012. In 2014 he was awarded two gold medals and received the title of Alabama Bartender of the Year. He has been the lead mixologist at The Hound in Auburn and director of beverage at the Depot Seafood Brasserie. Caleb is a Cicerone Certified Beer Server and a certified sommelier.

WINNER OF ALABAMA HOTEL AND RESTAURANT ALLIANCE'S 2014 BARTENDER OF THE YEAR COMPETITION 2014

CATHLÁIN NAOMH PHÁDRAIG
(SAINT PATRICK'S BATTALION)
BRIAN TODD

Brian says: *My cocktail was inspired by the infamous Irish bar scene.
I have sought to introduce quality tequilas to the Irish palate by pairing Patrón
with Guinness. The flavour profile speaks for my home and workplace.
The cool and refreshing cucumber and lime represents the cleansing Irish weather,
whilst the spicy notes of Patrón Reposado and dashes of Tabasco represent the
memorable and warm people of Belfast and Ireland. The remaining ingredients
bring an exciting, unexpected taste sensation.*

2 DASHES WHISKEY BARREL BITTERS
2 DASHES TABASCO
5ML AGAVE SEC LIQUEUR
50ML CUCUMBER AND LIME WATER*
50ML HOMEMADE GUINNESS REDUCTION**
50ML PATRÓN REPOSADO TEQUILA
1 EGG WHITE

METHOD: Add all the ingredients to the shaker in the order that they are listed above. Add a scoop of ice and shake well. Strain into a coupe glass and garnish with a viola flower.

CUCUMBER AND LIME WATER*
Add 1 cucumber and the juice of 3 limes to a blender. Blend until smooth, then strain through a muslin cloth to remove all the solids. Store in a sealed container in the fridge.

HOMEMADE GUINNESS REDUCTION**
Heat a bottle of Guinness in a pan until it has reduced by 75 per cent. Allow to cool and then refrigerate.

————

BRIAN TODD had never really intended to become a bartender. Like many in the bar industry, he entered it as a method of generating an income while focusing on his 'real' career. However, whilst the non-hospitality career was treading water somewhat, his obvious skills with people and mixing drinks propelled him to a point where he was climbing the mixology ladder at a much faster rate. And whilst Brian has been bartending in one form or another since 2014, he has only been bartending full-time since the middle of 2016, making his 2017 competition victory a quite remarkable achievement. His current position of head bartender at The Five Points plus his victory in the Patrón Perfectionist competition suggests that he is probably on the right career path now.

WINNER OF PATRÓN PERFECTIONIST COCKTAIL COMPETITION, IRELAND 2017

CINCO DE MAYO
TRINH QUAN HUY-PHILIP

Huy-Philip says: *Cinco de Mayo was inspired by the namesake celebration of the Mexican army's 1862 victory over France. Tequila as the base represents the Mexican nation. The Wenneker Strawberry represents the love of the Mexican people, and the raspberry gives freshness of flavour and the colour of the blood spilled. The red pepper provides the heat of despair of the French failure. The lemon juice is to give the right balance of a losing battle and the agave syrup represents the sweetness of the Mexican victory.*

45ML JOSE CUERVO BLANCO TEQUILA
15ML WENNEKER STRAWBERRY
15ML DUBONNET
15ML FRESH LEMON JUICE
1 BSP AGAVE SYRUP
¼ RED PEPPER
5 RASPBERRIES
10ML MESCAL, TO TOP UP

METHOD: Muddle the red pepper and raspberries together in a cocktail shaker. Add the remaining ingredients and a scoop of ice. Shake well and strain into a rocks glass filled with crushed ice. Add the mescal to the top and garnish with lemon peel, mixed berries and a sprig of mint. Finish with a pinch of ground black pepper.

———

TRINH QUAN HUY-PHILIP started out as a bar server in Chu Bar in Saigon. Here he got the mixing bug and decided, aged 20, to enrol in bartending school. After qualifying, Huy-Philip worked his way through a number of top Vietnamese bars including the Park Hyatt, Saigon where he began competing in cocktail competitions. He became Vietnamese Mixxit Master in 2011. This victory took him to Europe where he started to acquire European mixing techniques. He has subsequently had much success, including a victory at the Classic Cocktail Competition in Germany. Billed as the Vietnamese Travelling Mixologist, Huy-Philip is a major player on the European cocktail scene.

WINNER OF WENNEKER SWIZZLE MASTERS 2015

CLARITA
RAN VAN ONGEVALLE

Ran says: *The inspiration for my drink came from many things.*
First of all, it came from the Bacardi family and their heritage. I saw a lot of similarities
between Don Facundo and myself, and knowing that Facundo was a Spanish wine
merchant before having his own company was a sign that the use of sherry was meant
to be. Also, the use of salt, which is a reflection of the interests of the modern bartender.
It's a modern classic with progressive ingredients.

60ML BACARDI OCHO RUM
10ML NPU AMONTILLADO SHERRY
5ML CRÈME DE CACAO TEMPUS FUGIT
2 DASHES PERNOD ABSINTHE
1 DASH SALINE SOLUTION*

METHOD: Add all the ingredients to a mixing glass with a scoop of ice and stir for 10-12 seconds. Strain into a coupe glass and garnish with 3 drops of olive oil.

SALINE SOLUTION*
Dissolve 44g sea salt in 1 litre water.

————————

RAN VAN ONGEVALLE has had a short but spectacular career. His rise to global cocktail mixing dominance has come in just five short years. In 2012 he landed the position of bar manager at BAAR in Ghent, Belgium. One year later he became co-owner and head bartender at The Pharmacy Group, a position he still holds. On the competition front his results have been amazing. In 2014 he won Belgium's Best Bartender and Best Cocktail Bar awards, was champion at the Citadelle Cocktail Competition and also champion at the Thomas Henry Cocktail Competition. In 2017 he won the national Bacardi Legacy Competition for Belgium and then went on the become world champion by winning the Global Bacardi Legacy finals. Ran is also co-owner of 2 Birds & A Dash, a global cocktail and bar consultancy.

WINNER OF BACARDI LEGACY GLOBAL FINALS 2017 (WORLD CHAMPION)

CLERGYMAN MARTINI
BOO JING HENG

Jing says: *The concept of my drink was to evolve a gin and tonic into a martini as the ingredients are powerfully complementary to the base spirit of Tanqueray Ten gin. The grapefruit, lime and orange flavours represent key ingredients used in the making of Tanqueray No. Ten. The name is inspired by master distiller Charles Tanqueray himself. His father and grandfather were both clergymen and it was anticipated that Charles would follow suit. However, he decided to forge a different path as a gin distiller. The name is a nod to his world-changing decision.*

45ML TANQUERAY NO. TEN GIN
15ML GRAPEFRUIT TONIC REDUCTION*
5ML HOMEMADE LIME CORDIAL**

METHOD: Add all the ingredients to a shaker with a scoop of ice. Shake well and strain into a martini glass. Garnish with a dehydrated lime wheel and orange zest***.

GRAPEFRUIT TONIC REDUCTION*
Boil plain tonic water until it has reduced by 75% (to a quarter of its volume). For every 15ml tonic reduction, add 1 dash grapefruit bitters.

HOMEMADE LIME CORDIAL**
Combine the grated zest of 2 limes, 18g citric acid, 300g caster sugar and 300ml hot water. Stir together until the sugar has dissolved, then seal in a container and keep in the fridge for 24 hours.

DEHYDRATED LIME WHEEL AND ORANGE ZEST***
Slice the lime wheel, shave the orange zest and place both on a baking tray. Place in an oven at very low heat (50–75°C) and bake until dry and crisp, usually 10–20 minutes.

BOO JING HENG is definitely a popular and well-respected personality within the bartending industry. He first discovered his interest in bartending while working part time at establishments such as Cafe Del Mar, where he picked up bartending techniques and skills on the job. At just 26 years old, Jing has already demonstrated his competitive accomplishments. In 2014, his first competition year, he achieved a third and two second places in global competitions including the Vedrenne Cocktail Grand Prix. The following year he swept the board in the Diageo World Class South East Asia finals by becoming the Classic Five Star Challenge Champion, the Bar Team Champion (Team Singapore), recipient of the Rising Star Award and the overall first runner-up, a position he exceeded when becoming the overall champion the following year. His latest accolade was winning the Asia Bar Battle at the 2017 Singapore Cocktail Week Festival.

WINNER OF DIAGEO WORLD CLASS SINGAPORE 2016

COCO BONG
MADHAN KUMAR

Madhan says: *The coconut tree is the national tree of the Maldives.*
It grows on every island and the locals use every single part of it. The 'mudi kaashi'
as it is called, is a soft, semi-sweet, white, round substance that is formed inside the
coconut once it has fallen to the ground and begun to germinate. It has a delicious
taste, but is not often used. Along with the mudi kaashi I have added coconut water
to the cocktail, which is known for its health benefits.

2CM PIECE OF MUDI KAASHI
40ML DANZKA VODKA
20ML VANILLA LIQUEUR
120ML COCONUT WATER

METHOD: Muddle the mudi kaashi in the cocktail shaker until it is smooth. Add the remaining ingredients and a scoop of ice and shake well. Double strain into a small glass bottle.

FLAIR-BARTENDER*: The guys you see juggling bottles like Tom Cruise did in the film *Cocktail*... although much better!

MADHAN KUMAR has been working in top-class hotels in the Maldives since 2006. He is also one of very few flair-bartenders* included in this book, having competed in and won the state Flair-Bartending Competition in 2006. On the mixology front, Madhan has placed in the top three in multiple national cocktail championships between 2006 and 2016. As yet without a major competition win, we felt that Madhan's experience alongside his fabulous drink was something that we wanted to share with you. Madhan can currently be found tending bar on cruise ships sailing out of Australia.

WINNER OF MALDIVES NATIONAL COCKTAIL COMPETITION 2015 (2ND PLACE)

CRIOLLO

ANTONIO NARANJO NEVARES

Antonio says: *The inspiration for my cocktail came from
the word criollo, colloquially meaning of 'good blend'.
Criollo is the name given to a person of pure Spanish descent living on
the American continent and of the highest social caste.*

50ML HAVANA 7-YEAR-OLD RUM
25ML AFRICAN RUBY ROOIBOS VERMOUTH
10ML SHERRY
200ML UMESHU

METHOD: Add all the ingredients to a mixing glass with a scoop of ice and stir it for 15 seconds. Strain in to an ice-filled rocks glass and garnish with a twist of orange.

———————

ANTONIO NARANJO NEVARES began working with cocktails at 41 Degrees of Parallel Street, one of the most famous venues in Spain and sibling to the world famous El Bulli. He's a highly accomplished mixologist, with his amazing creations taking first place in multiple competitions including the national Domaine de Canton competition. He has also represented Spain in the Bacardi Global Legacy competition. In addition to the competitions, he is involved with a number of major international events like the 50 Best Bars Awards and has also been a judge at the Bacardi Legacy National Competition. Antonio was the bar chief at the prestigious Alfonso XIII Hotel and a tutor at Taberna del Alabardero hotel school in Seville. He is now a partner and bar manager in the local Dr. Stravinsky, a new concept bar based in his home country of Spain.

CUBAN PETE

INGRID SKAUE ØINES

Ingrid says: *Cuban Pete is about the fun and joy of the hospitality industry and is a refreshing cocktail, made for anyone to enjoy. My motivation for taking part in Bacardi Legacy and creating Cuban Pete was to set the focus on the personalities we meet across the bar; to create memories, experiences; to entertain and share stories. Cuban Pete is about having fun!*

50ML BACARDI CARTA BLANCA RUM
20ML WHITE CRÈME DE CACAO
20ML COCONUT WATER
20ML FRESH LIME JUICE
6–8 FRESH MINT LEAVES

METHOD: Add all the ingredients (including the mint leaves) to a shaker with a scoop of ice. Shake hard and strain into a coupe glass. Garnish with lime zest and extra mint leaves.

————

INGRID SKAUE ØINES is a person of many talents. She is a former professional dancer (11 years), a talented photographer and, of course, a highly skilled mixologist. Although her hospitality career dates back to 2008, it wasn't until 2014 that she found her calling on the bar. Within one year of discovering her talents for bartending and mixology, she reached the finals of Norwegian Beefeater Mixldn and Scandinavian Nikka Perfect Serve competitions, getting into the top 10 on both occasions, both truly impressive achievements considering the short time spent on the bar. This rapid competition success encouraged her to work even harder on the development of her skills and two years on she won the Norwegian Bacardi Legacy Competition 2017, going on to represent her country in the global finals.

WINNER OF BACARDI LEGACY NORWAY 2017

CUPPA JOVE

JACK ALEXANDER (SOTTI) SOTIRIOU

Jack says: *The cocktail was designed for Salvatore Calabrese.*
I wanted to show the old Italian how we Aussies can play with the fruity flavours
of coffee. I wanted to emphasise the citrus notes with a full-bodied gin and Amaro.
The cocktail itself was named after Charles Hawtrey's infamous quote upon
tasting that drink for the first time, 'By Jove, that's Hanky Panky!'

45ML TANQUERAY NO. TEN GIN

15ML OLOROSO SHERRY

15ML FIG LIQUEUR

5ML AMARO BRANCA MENTA

5ML SUGAR SYRUP

2 DASHES ABSINTHE

1.5G FRESHLY GROUND ARABICA COFFEE

METHOD: Add all ingredients to shaker with a scoop of ice. Throw ingredients from one tin to another to aerate and dilute. Strain into a coffee aeropress and extract the coffee from the cocktail. Strain into a double-walled glass and garnish with a mandarin twist.

————————

JACK ALEXANDER SOTIRIOU's career began as a host for a series of venues in Leeds. A year later, on his 19th birthday, he made the decision to transfer to the bar and learn the art of 'craft' bartending. A move to New Zealand followed, where he 'blagged' a job on his first night by turning up at the 1885 cocktail bar and nightclub, claiming he had been booked to do a trial shift. A year later he was the venue manager! It was here that his mentor, Alan Raythorn, encouraged him to enter competitions. Six competitions and two years later, Jack (along with Alan) moved to Melbourne to further his career. He entered numerous additional competitions and got his first big title with Ketel One's Best Bloody Mary, Australia competition. Jack then went on to win Bols Around the World, Australia. By 2015, Jack was the general manager at the Boilermaker House, during which time he represented Australia in the Global World Class finals, finishing 'on the podium' with a third place overall. Jack is now part owner of Boilermaker House.

DÉJÀ VU
VITĚZSLAV CIROK

Vitězslav says: The moment you taste my Déjà Vu cocktail it reminds you of something from your past. For me, it's Paris in the spring and summer and so that is where the name came from.

35ML CIROC VODKA

10ML SUZE

20ML VERJUS (MOSCATEL)

3 DASHES ST. ANTOINE ABSINTHE (CZECH PRODUCER)

30ML GOOSEBERRY AND ELDERFLOWER SODA

METHOD: Add all the ingredients to a mixing glass with a scoop of ice and stir until chilled and blended. Strain into a goblet glass and garnish with an edible flower (or grape).

————

VITĚZSLAV CIROK has been bartending since 2004 when he got his first taste of the bar as a bar-back in one of Prague's many nightclubs. Over time he worked as a bartender in various restaurants, clubs and hotels, but it wasn't until he landed a job at the Cloud9 hotel bar that he 'fell in love' with mixology. Vitezslav took his new-found passion for cocktails to a new job at a club called Phenomen, where his team was awarded the Best Club award on multiple occasions. The year 2015 turned out to be Vitězslav's best year to date. Not only did he win the national Diageo World Class event, he was also named Czech Bartender of the Year by the Czech Bartending Association. In addition, he represented his country in the Diageo World Class Global Finals where he finished a highly impressive sixth in the world.

DISAROLLYWOOD

FRANCESCO CIONE

Francesco says: *This drink gets its inspiration from the 2012 Bollywood theme of The Mixing Star global competition. Well-known Indian ingredients, like mango and cardamom, marry together with the round sweet character of Disaronno. The fizzy kick of the carbonated cranberry juice gives a nice vibrant taste, which can be compared to the sparkling 'song-and-dance' attitude of the Bollywood scene. The Mixing Stars infusion represents the magic behind every Indian and American movie, a true protagonist for this drink with a fancy signature 'portmanteau' name: Disarollywood.*

40ML DISARONNO ORIGINALE
20ML CARDAMOM SYRUP
15ML FRESH LIME JUICE
50ML MANGO JUICE
45ML CARBONATED CRANBERRY JUICE*

METHOD: Chill a fancy cocktail glass and a shaker tin, both filled with ice. To another shaker tin, add all the ingredients, except the cranberry juice. Mix everything by rolling it with the Indian 'Chai Tea' technique, also know as 'Cuban throwing' (pouring the liquid from the shaker tin with ice to the other one for four or five times). Then strain everything into the fancy glass with ice and fill up with the Carbonated Cranberry Juice from a soda syphon. Garnish with lime, dried wild rose and lemongrass and serve the drink on a little tray with a side of 'Mixing Stars'**.

CARBONATED CRANBERRY JUICE*
Fill up a soda syphon with enough cranberry juice and charge it with Co2. Keep in the fridge for a couple of hours.

MIXING STARS**
Steep kaffir lime leaves, dry wild roses, lime, grapefruit and oranges in hot water during the cocktail making. Pour the infusion over dry ice, which will dissolve all the fragrances and scent around the drink.

————————

FRANCESCO CIONE describes himself as a passionate 'Lovetender'. Francesco was born into the hospitality industry as his family have owned the legendary Dallas Bar in Verbania, Italy since 1980. He has worked at the American and Lounge bars on the 'lake', then went on to Geneva and Leeds before moving in to the 'super-luxury' end of the market in hotels like the Cipriani in Venice. In 2008 he won the Angelo Zola prize at the AIBES National Cocktail Competition as Best Bartender of the Year. In addition, Francesco won the Perfect Bartender Challenge in 2013, and Diageo World Class Italy in 2015.

WINNER OF DISARONNO, THE MIXING STAR GLOBAL COCKTAIL COMPETITION 2012

THE DOORKNOBS
GIACOMO VEZZO

Giacomo says: *My drink is inspired by* Alice in Wonderland *so I decided to serve the cocktail in a teapot. I wanted to draw on the words used by the doorknob when Alice attempted to open the door. It said, 'Oooh it's impassible, not impossible, nothing is impossible'. Doorknobs therefore became the name of my signature cocktail. With the Hendrick's botanic flavours and a pleasant sweet and sour aftertaste, it's perfect as an any-time-of-the-day cocktail, especially at teatime!*

100ML HENDRICK'S GIN
40ML CARPANO BIANCO
2 TBSP ORGANIC ROSE MARMALADE
20ML FRESH LEMON JUICE
A SPLASH OF SODA
ELDERFLOWER TONIC, TO TOP UP

METHOD: Add the first four ingredients to a shaker and dry shake with 1 cube of ice until the marmalade is completely blended. Now pour into a teapot half-filled with ice. Add the soda and top with the elderflower tonic. Serve in a teacup garnished with a rose petal.

———

GIACOMO VEZZO is an archetypal international bartender, having tended bar over a ten-year period in Solerno, Ibiza, London, Paris and Dubai, where he is currently the bar manager of the prestigious Buddha Bar at the Grosvenor House Hotel, Starwood Marriott. Giacomo was the winner of the 2014 San Pellegrino 'Flash Contest' and came second in his first attempt at the Hendrick's Cup in 2015. In 2016, alongside winning the Hendrick's Cup, he made the final of the Glenfiddich Most Experimental Bartender competition. That same year, Jagermeister appointed him their brand ambassador for the Berlin Bartender Contest, which was followed in 2017 by dual success in the Diageo World Class 2017, where he placed second in the Simplicity vs Eccentricity category before going on to win the Coffee category.

DUTCH IN ASIA
AMIT SOOD

Amit says: *This cocktail was inspired by my love of the Martini/Gibson cocktail, my background work as a chef, and my love of Thai cuisine after travelling there for two months.*

60ML KETEL ONE VODKA
5ML NOILLY PRAT

METHOD: Add the ingredients to a mixing glass with lots of ice and stir for 30 seconds. Strain into a chilled martini/coupe glass and garnish with my homemade Sood Onions*.

SOOD ONIONS*
To a pan, add the following ingredients: 1 litre rice vinegar, 25g yellow lump rock sugar, 5 star anise, 5 dried red bird's eye chillies, 1 tbsp coriander seeds, 1 tsp fennel seeds, 30g fresh ginger root, 1 tbsp Szechuan peppercorns, 25ml soy sauce and 1 tbsp sea salt. Gently heat, then add 30 peeled Thai shallots and continue to warm for 30 minutes. Turn off the heat and leave to cool. Once cool, transfer to a sterilised jar and keep in fridge.

NOTE FROM PAUL: *This recipe demonstrates exactly how Amit's creative mind works. In essence, it is a Gibson cocktail (a martini served with a cocktail onion instead of an olive). However, instead of trying to alter the alcoholic ingredients, Amit decide to focus his creative efforts on developing a recipe for the onion. As a Gibson drinker myself, I can tell you that it's well worth the effort.*

AMIT SOOD has been at the centre of the UK bar scene for over two decades. As a bartending purist, he made an early decision not to enter competitions, choosing instead to focus on spreading 'the word' and helping others to achieve their goals. This is not to say he hasn't created many hundreds of unique recipes. In fact, it's his wonderfully creative approach that resulted in him being recognised as a cocktail innovator earlier in 2017. In his early years, Amit bartended for some of the biggest organisations of the 1990s and early noughties, including, TGI Fridays, Maxwell's, Navajo Joe and Sticky Fingers. As his career progressed he became bar manager at the prestigious Purple Bar at The Sanderson, event manager for Behind Bars and senior event manager for Create Cocktails. Since 2007, Amit has dedicated himself to delivering high-class training – he was a consultant trainer for The Training School (industry-focused training company), and from 2009-2016 was director of training for Shaker UK. He is currently head of training for the Maxxium drinks company.

WINNER OF MIXXA CLASSIC COCKTAIL INNOVATION 2017

EL COMIENZO PERFECTO
CHELSIE BAILEY

Chelsie Says: *My inspiration was taken from one of the beginning elements of agave spirits, 'pulque', similar to a milky, yeast-like beer. I wanted to take the young vegetal yet richer flavours of the Patrón Reposado tequila and essentially make a modern-day pulque using tequila and beer. Influenced by Mexican flavours, the goddess Mayahuel and Patrón's quest for perfection, I have created a drink that is perfect to enjoy in the Mexican heat.*

45ML PATRÓN REPOSADO TEQUILA
20ML PINEAPPLE SHERBET*
15ML CREAM
15ML FRESH LIME JUICE
15ML EGG WHITE
30ML MEXICAN LAGER

METHOD: Add all the ingredients except the Mexican lager to a shaker and dry shake (no ice). Add the ice and shake again. Strain into a frozen fizz glass and top with the lager. Garnish with pineapple leaves and dehydrated chilli.

PINEAPPLE SHERBET*
Roast a whole pineapple at 180ºC for 20 minutes. Chop the pineapple into chunks, removing the skin and core, and add to a blender. Season with fresh chilli, coriander, clove and anise to taste and blend until smooth. Store in an airtight container in the fridge.

———

CHELSIE BAILEY is a Bristol-based bartender. Over a ten-year period she has worked mainly in the UK with a short stint at the Town Hall Hotel in Melbourne, Australia. Since 2015 she has been the head bartender at the Red Light Bar in Bristol, helping them to achieve the Best Bar Team and Best Cocktail Bar awards at the Bristol Cocktail Awards 2015. Chelsie has a genuine flair for cocktail creation, and as such has taken to competing in a range of high-profile cocktail competitions since 2014, with hugely impressive results. In a short space of time she has won four competitions, including the National Appleton Estate Bartender Challenge. Her most recent achievements include winning the Posh Pen to Shaker European competition, being named as Bristol Best Bartender of the Year 2016 and becoming the UK Monkey Shoulder UBC champion.

WINNER OF PATRÓN PERFECTIONISTS COCKTAIL COMPETITION, BRISTOL 2017

EL TACO ROJO
JENNIFER LE NECHET

Jennifer says: *It's a cocktail inspired by Mexican tacos. Like in a taco, I wanted to highlight the taste of the corn, so I infused the Don Julio Blanco in a sous vide machine at low temperature to keep all the brightness and ABV from the Don Julio and to extract the taste of the corn. Then I add a red bell pepper shrub made of cider vinegar and white balsamic cream, and a homemade soda based on citrus and basil.*

60ML DON JULIO BLANCO INFUSED WITH GRILLED CORN*
30ML RED BELL PEPPER SHRUB**
60ML HOMEMADE CITRUS AND BASIL SODA***
BESPOKE RIM OF SALT AND SPICES FROM SOUTHERN FRANCE

METHOD: Add all the ingredients to a cocktail shaker with a scoop of ice. Shake well and strain into a ceramic taco-shaped vessel (or you can use a regular tumbler). Garnish with some basil leaves.

DON JULIO BLANCO INFUSED WITH GRILLED CORN*
Combine 500ml Don Julio with 75g grilled corn in a sous vide machine at 58°C for 2 hours. Alternatively, if you don't have access to a sous vide machine, seal the ingredients in a water-tight bag and gently warm in a pan of water at low temperature (using a thermometer to get as close to 58°C as possible).

RED BELL PEPPER SHRUB**
Put 500ml fresh red bell-pepper juice in a pan, add 800g white sugar and heat until the sugar has dissolved. Filter the mixture, then add 350ml cider vinegar and 150ml white balsamic cream.

HOMEMADE CITRUS AND BASIL SODA***
Add 50ml fresh lime juice, 10 basil leaves, 1 tsp mixed spice and a chopped red bell pepper to 250ml water and allow to infuse. Strain the liquid, then charge in a soda syphon.

JENNIFER LE NECHET is truly one of the world's finest current mixologists. Living and working in Paris, France, she has been bartending since 2009. In an exceptional year in 2016 she received the title of Best Bartender in the World and became the Global winner of Diageo World Class, having naturally won the French Diageo competition to qualify. Since her amazing success, she has combined her full-time job as head bartender of the Modern Café in Paris with her new role as the World Class ambassador. This role sees Jennifer conducting cocktail master-classes, judging national and international competitions, collaborating on the creation of new events and appearing as a 'guest bartender' in establishments around the world.

ELIXIR TROPICAL
MAURIZIO LA SPINA

Maurizio says: *The inspiration for my drink comes from a simple question: What really is a 'tropical cocktail'? In my view, it's an 'elixir' with the power to transport you to a tropical island. It is a vacation in your glass! That's why I created a cocktail evocative of Cuba during the great golden age of tropical cocktails. This is where the keystone of tropical mixology was born, the holy trinity of cocktails, the Daiquiri.*

60ml Bacardi Carta Blanca Rum
20ml fresh lime juice
20ml orgeat syrup
7.5ml Maraschino Luxardo
2–3 medium mint leaves
3 dashes Angostura Bitters

METHOD: Add all the ingredients to a shaker with a scoop of ice. Shake hard and fine strain into a coupe glass. Garnish with freshly grated nutmeg sprinkled on top.

————————

MAURIZIO LA SPINA was born in Naples, one of the most famous cities in the world for hospitality and food. During his career he worked as head bartender at Billionaire, one of the most exclusive clubs in Europe, in Porto Cervo, Sardinia. As a result of this high-level experience, he was recruited to tend bar alongside the F1 Grand Prix tour and worked in some amazing venues from the Fairmont Hotel in Monte Carlo to Baku in Azerbaijan. Currently, Maurizio works at his own bartender training school in Naples. He is a great lover of the Tiki style of cocktail and created the Tiki-based Marama Project that unites Italian bartenders and artists across Italy at dedicated events. He has also collaborated with various Italian ceramicists to create his own line of unique Tiki mugs. Maurizio's win at the Italian Bacardi Legacy Cocktail Competition in 2017 is his career competitive highlight.

ENDLESS SUMMER
MICHAEL NORAT

Michael says: *My Endless Summer cocktail represents my beautiful island. It reflects our culture, the availability of wonderful ingredients, the people and the warm welcome afforded to everybody. This is my favourite creation because it also represents my hard work and dedication to my craft.*

25ML ZACAPA 23 RUM
25ML RON DEL BARRILITO DE PUERTO RICO
18ML FRESH LEMON JUICE
18ML FALERNUM
3 CARAMELISED PINEAPPLE CUBES*
3 DASHES ANGOSTURA BITTERS
CARBONATED GINGER TEA**

METHOD: Add all the ingredients except the tea to a shaker and muddle together. Add a scoop of ice and shake hard. Double strain into a cocktail glass, top up with the Carbonated Ginger Tea and garnish with a slice of pineapple and pineapple leaves.

CARAMELISED PINEAPPLE CUBES*
Roll pineapple cubes in brown sugar, then heat them with a blowtorch until golden brown (you can place them under a hot grill as an alternative).

CARBONATED GINGER TEA**
Brew 250ml ginger tea and allow to cool. Charge in a soda syphon just before serving.

_____

MICHAEL NORAT was born to bartend. In fact, you could say that it's in his blood as his father, uncle and grandfather have worked in and owned bars in cities like New York and Miami. His formal career started at the ABC Bartending School in Miami when he was just 18. Thereafter, upon returning to Puerto Rico he worked at the Bistro de Paris where he began experimenting with European methods of mixology. In 2008 and 2009 Michael began winning regional cocktail competitions which led to him travelling to countries like France and Spain, where he had the opportunity to gain a more 'global vision' of cocktail mixology. Michael describes his current bar as his 'laboratory', where he continually challenges his own skills and ideas in a quest to deliver ever-evolving cocktail experiences for his guests.

WINNER OF DIAGEO WORLD CLASS PUERTO RICO 2015

34

ENTANGLED
LUDOVICA (LULU) FEDI

Lulu says: *I took inspiration from two of my favourite artists,
Frida Kahlo and Josephine Baker. To me they embody strength and resilience with
a lot of fun and energy. The excitement and energy is conveyed in the cocktail.*

50ML PATRÓN REPOSADO TEQUILA
25ML BANANA LEAF AND GINGER-INFUSED BANANA LIQUEUR*
25ML FRESH LIME JUICE
3 DASHES GINGER BITTERS
75ML TURMERIC SODA**

METHOD: Fill a highball glass with ice, then add the first four ingredients in the order they are listed. Stir together, add more ice if required (to the top of the glass) and finish off with the Turmeric Soda. Garnish with a banana leaf.

BANANA LEAF AND GINGER-INFUSED
BANANA LIQUEUR*
Combine 500ml banana liqueur with 50g sliced root ginger and a chopped banana leaf. Allow to infuse for 48 hours, then strain and keep chilled.

TURMERIC SODA**
Begin by making a tumeric syrup: combine 2 tsp ground turmeric with 300g white sugar and 225ml water. Heat in a pan until the sugar has dissolved, then allow to cool and chill. For the soda, add 100ml of the turmeric syrup and 700ml water to a soda syphon and charge with a C02 charger.

LULU FEDI began her hospitality career in 2009 as a food-runner at the famous Soho House in London. Within two years, Lulu had graduated to the position of bartender at the Hide Bar in Bermondsey Street and within another two had become the bar supervisor there. In 2013, Lulu made a trip to Hong Kong where she spent a year focusing on the development of her cocktail-mixing skills. Since her return to the UK in 2014, she has held a variety of high-level roles including her most recent as head bartender of the American Bar at the Gleneagles Hotel in Scotland. In addition to her bartending career, since 2015 she has been the brand ambassador for Distilleries et Domains de Provence in the UK.

WINNER OF PATRÓN PERFECTIONIST COCKTAIL COMPETITION, SCOTLAND 2017

35

ENVY ME
NICK WU

Nick says: *I get inspiration for my cocktails from many places.*
Sometimes I take the craziest flavours I can think of and mix them together
without thinking whether it would make sense. Sometimes I also take
food elements that nobody has ever thought of using in cocktails,
and put them into a new drink. Talking to and working with people from
all walks of life is another thing that greatly inspires me.

55ML TANQUERAY NO. TEN GIN
10ML GREEN TEA LIQUEUR
10ML NOILLY PRAT AMBER
20ML GREEN SOY SYRUP
10ML FRESH LIME JUICE
20ML EGG WHITE

METHOD: Add all the ingredients to a shaker with a scoop of ice and shake well. Strain into a coupe glass and garnish with a green soy bean pod.

———————

NICK WU has more than a decade of experience, and is known to be one of the pioneers of Taiwan's bartending scene. He started out at the famed TGI Fridays and became one of the best flair-tenders in the region. In 2007, he broke onto the global scene when he won the Asia Pacific Flare Championship in Melbourne. Nick rode the cocktail boom and started his own consultancy and training company, which has helped to organise the inaugural Taiwan Bar Show. In 2015, Nick founded East End Bar Taipei. Nick found 2016 to be a year of great achievements: he placed third in the Diageo World Class Global Final in Miami where he was the champion of two categories – the Before and After – Aperitif and Digestif, and the American Classics Speed Round.

WINNER OF DIAGEO WORLD CLASS GLOBAL, SPEED ROUND 2016

EVENING SURPRISE

HENRY 'ALE' SIKTIMU

Henry says: *The inspiration for my drink is as follows: One evening a guest came to the bar and said that he wanted to drink a cocktail that tasted like a Negroni but was something different! 'Surprise me!', he said. So... I took the basic ingredients from The Dutchie, replacing the mint with Thai basil and, to add the bitter character, I included a long bar spoon of Campari. The guest was very happy and had an amazing surprise.*

2 x 3cm pieces coriander root
6–8 Thai basil leaves
60ml London No.3 Dry Gin
30ml fresh lemon juice
20ml tamarillo syrup
5ml Campari
1 dash orange bitters
Cardamom Soda*, to top up

METHOD: First, chill your sherry flute with ice. Add the coriander root to the shaker and muddle. Take the Thai basil, slap between your hands (to release the oils) and add to the coriander. Now add all the remaining ingredients except the soda. Add a scoop of ice and shake hard. Discard the ice from the sherry flute and double strain into it. Top with the Cardamom Soda (approx. 20ml) and serve.

CARDAMOM SODA*
Boil 100ml water in a pan and add 20g green cardamom pods. Simmer for 10-15 minutes, then strain into a jar. Allow to cool. When you are ready to use, add the liquid to a soda syphon and charge. Chill the syphon in the fridge for 5-10 minutes before serving.

————————

HENRY SIKTIMU has been working the Indonesian bar scene for more than ten years. In that time he has tended bar at many of Jakarta's top establishments and has established a reputation for creating 'outrageous' cocktail recipes. He began competing in competitions in 2015 having attained a level that he believed worthy of competition. His first competition was Diageo World Class Indonesia 2015, where he reached the semi-final stage, a feat he repeated the following year. Also in 2015, he achieved his first win when he became national champion in the Indonesia, London No. 3 Gin Cocktail Competition. In 2016 he was recognised for Best Performance in the Teisseire Cocktail Competition, which was followed by his best Diageo result so far when he reached the top 3 in the 2017 World Class event.

WINNER OF LONDON No. 3 GIN COCKTAIL COMPETITION 2016

EVEREST
GAZ (GARY) REGAN

Gaz says: *Tea is one of the botanicals used in Beefeater 24 gin,
and tea got me thinking about India. India made me think of curry, and curry
made me think of Thai curry. That's where the coconut/curry paste idea came from.
The Everest was the name of an absolutely fabulous – though very much hole-in-the-wall
– Indian restaurant in Blackpool, England, where I used to go for late-night
vindaloos in the early 1970s. That's where the name came from.*

75ML BEEFEATER 24 GIN
22.5ML COCONUT CURRY PASTE*
15ML FRESH LEMON JUICE

METHOD: Add all the ingredients to a cocktail shaker with a scoop of ice. Shake and strain into a chilled cocktail glass. Sprinkle a pinch of curry powder over the surface of the drink to garnish.

COCONUT CURRY PASTE*
Mix 1 tsp curry powder with 45ml Coco Lopez to make a paste. Store in the refrigerator.

NOTE FROM PAUL: *Gaz has never entered (and therefore never won) a competition. However, he is one of the most influential bartenders of all time and his creations are sensational. Therefore, we have decided to include him and give you all the chance of sampling his genius!*

GAZ REGAN is without doubt one of the most influential mixologists of all time. Gaz wrote 'The Cocktailian', a regular column for the *San Francisco Chronicle* for 13 years and publishes five weekly newsletters that reach over 50,000 bartenders and cocktail enthusiasts worldwide. Between 1991 and 2009 he wrote 12 books, including the revered *Bartender's Bible* and *The Joy of Mixology*. Three editions of *Gaz Regan's Annual Manual for Bartenders* have been published between 2011 and 2014, and Gaz's *101 Best New Cocktails* is a book published annually. He also conducts Cocktails in the Country, a series of two-day bartender workshops in New York. Gaz has been awarded and recognised at the very highest level, including being named Best Cocktail Writer in 2008, and receiving the Helen David Lifetime Achievement Award in 2012 and the Best Cocktail Writing Award in 2013. He was also inducted into the Kentucky Bourbon Hall of Fame in 2004 and has been listed as one of the Top Ten Bartenders Throughout History by *The Spirits Business* magazine. In 2015, Gaz published *The Negroni: Drinking to La Dolce Vita*.

38

FANCY NANCY
(THE OLD FLAME)
DALE DEGROFF

Dale says: *I did a cocktail dinner on the road...I think it was in Texas ...
actually I did several at Rainbow in the 1990s and got a sort of reputation for matching
cocktails and courses with chefs. [For the rest of this fascinating story turn to page 202.
Not enough room to tell it here... thanks Dale!]*

30ML GIN
30ML COINTREAU
15ML ITALIAN SWEET VERMOUTH
15ML CAMPARI
30ML FRESH ORANGE JUICE

METHOD: Add all the ingredients to a shaker with a scoop of ice. Shake well and strain into a chilled martini glass. Garnish by flaming an orange zest over the top and dropping it in the drink.

———————

DALE DEGROFF is arguably the biggest name in the world of cocktails. So much so, he is known by the respected moniker of 'King Cocktail'. Dale developed his extraordinary techniques and talent for tending bar at the legendary Rainbow Room in New York. His industry awards include the 2009 James Beard Wine & Spirits Professional Award, the 2009 Lifetime Achievement Award from *Nightclub & Bar* magazine, the 2008 Tales of the Cocktail Lifetime Achievement Award, and the 2007 Cheers Beverage Industry Innovator of the Year with his partners, for Beverage Alcohol Resource. Dale is the author two best-selling, award-winning cocktail books: *The Essential Cocktail* and *The Craft of the Cocktail*. He is also the founding President of The Museum of the American Cocktail. His other passions include singing (note: I can attest to that) and storytelling. As such, Dale has performed his one man show, *On the Town – Bars, Speaks and Legendary Saloons*, in over 30 cities in the US and overseas. With this drink, Dale introduced the world to the flamed orange peel zest that is now used by bartenders globally when serving a Cosmopolitan.

WINNER OF BACARDI MARTINI GRAND PRIX 2001

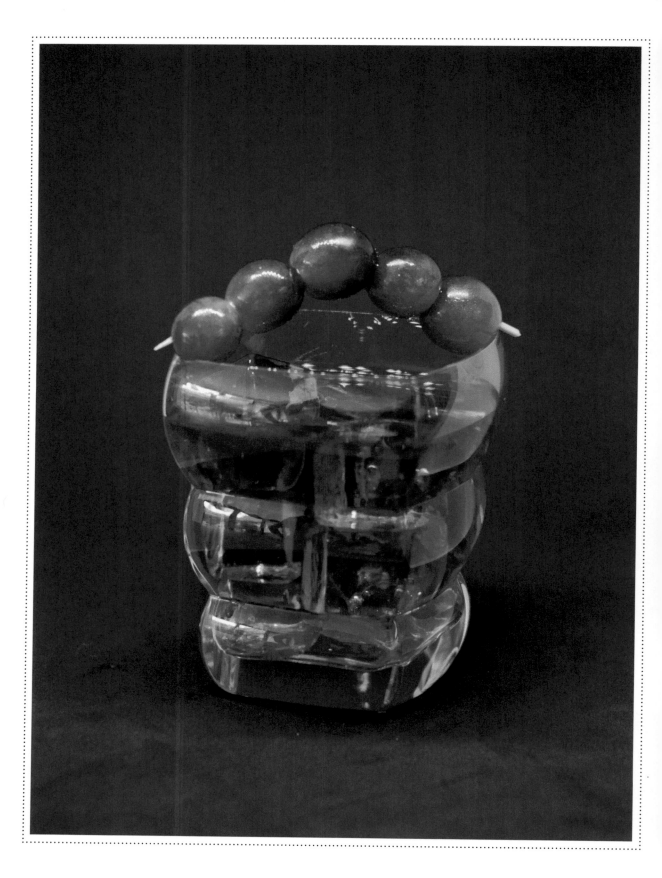

39

FLOR DE JALISCO

FELIX H. CUEVAS

Felix says: *My drink is inspired by the love that Don Julio always dedicated to his family and the passion he has always had to work. And it is from here, from these details, that Flor de Jalisco (Flowers of Jalisco) is born. Because for Don Julio the most important flowers in his life were his children and, in his garden, his pineapple agave.*

50ML DON JULIO REPOSADO TEQUILA
60ML WHITE GRAPE JUICE
15ML HOMEMADE SIROPE DE GRANADA* (OR YOU CAN USE GRENADINE)

METHOD: Chill the shaker by adding a scoop of ice, shaking, and then discarding the ice. Now add the ingredients and shake for 10 seconds in the chilled shaker without ice (this is known as a 'dry shake'). Now pour into a chilled old-fashioned glass filled with ice. Garnish with grapes on a bamboo cocktail stick.

HOMEMADE SIROPE DE GRANADA*
Heat the seeds of 1 pomegranate with 250g caster sugar until the pomegranate seeds release their juice and the sugar melts (do not allow to come to the boil). If the mixture is too stiff, add a little water. When the liquid is a deep red colour, allow to cool, strain, bottle and keep chilled.

FELIX CUEVAS has been bartending since 1997 and has spent his career to date in Panama. He currently works as chief mixologist for the company 2cocktails, a bar-training consultancy, is an instructor at the Bartenders Training Academy, works as brand mixologist for Diageo Panama (a result of his World Class victory), and is a regular on the judging panel for many of Panama's cocktail competitions.
As a competitive mixologist, Felix has had considerable success. In 2015 he won the Diplomatic World Cocktail Tournament and Diageo World Class Panama. He then went on to become Best Mixologist 2016 as awarded by *Ocean Drive* magazine, and in 2017 received the World Distinction from Worldchefs in recognition of his success in bringing Panamanian mixology to a global audience.

WINNER OF DIAGEO WORLD CLASS PANAMA 2015

FOR NONO
CHRIS CHAMBERLAIN

Chris says: *Given the secret ingredient of rhubarb for the 'Aperitif' category, I wanted to pay homage to my wife's grandfather in Sicily ('nono' in the title is Italian for grandpa). Upon our last visit, before he passed, we sipped upon Americano cocktails, while eating fresh blood oranges around a camp fire. Thus, I wanted to recreate that experience in the glass by merging those classic flavours with the rhubarb, and adding the hickory-smoked Luxardo cherry to create the aroma of sitting around the fire on that beautiful day.*

28ML CARPANO ANTICA FORMULA
28ML LILLET ROSE VERMOUTH
7ML SOLERNO BLOOD ORANGE LIQUEUR
7ML FRESHLY EXTRACTED RHUBARB JUICE
1 BSP RHUBARB JAM
A SPLASH OF FEVER TREE TONIC

METHOD: Add all the ingredients except the tonic to a cocktail shaker with a scoop of ice and shake vigorously. Uncap the shaker and add a splash of tonic. Double strain into a double old-fashioned rocks glass filled with fresh ice. Garnish with a rhubarb spear and a hickory-smoked Luxardo cherry.

———

CHRIS CHAMBERLAIN has over two decades' experience of the drinks industry and is the National Beverage Development Manager for the E. & J. Gallo Spirits portfolio. Chris has played an intricate role in the development, activation and judging of many prestigious cocktail competitions. Among his many roles, Chris is a member of the United States Bartenders Guild and has achieved multiple accolades in the world of mixology, including many for his efforts in the WSWA (Wine and Spirits Wholesalers of America) Call for Cocktails competitions. In addition to his win at the 2013 Iron Mixologist competition, his cocktails have been featured in various trade and media publications, and he has also presented cocktail seminars at major events like the world-renowned Epcot Food and Wine Show and Bar Convent in Berlin.

WINNER OF IRON MIXOLOGIST 2013

FOREST BLOOM

GUSTAVO WIEZBOLOWSKI

Gustavo says: I won the Israeli National Bartending competition in
July 2004 and the prize was to be the Israeli competitor at the IBA World Championship
for the first time ever (Israel had just been accepted as a new member).
The task was to make three copies of an original cocktail in 5 minutes and relate
the cocktail to the music from a movie scene, and even wear a costume while
doing the performance. I made a movie scene from The Matrix.

40ML MARIE BRIZARD ANISETTE LIQUEUR
20ML MARIE BRIZARD CASSIS DE BORDEAUX
10ML MONIN BLACKBERRY SYRUP
10ML FRESH LEMON JUICE

METHOD: Add all the ingredients to a shaker with a scoop of ice. Shake well and strain into an ice-filled goblet. Garnish with fresh wild fruits, lemon peel and 2 star anise.

———————

GUSTAVO WIEZBOLOWSKI was born in Argentina and moved to Israel in 1999. Having begun working as a chef, in 2001 Gustavo's boss said to him, 'Change your clothes, we need you in the pub'! That was in the King Solomon Hotel – it was his first ever bar shift and, as it transpired, the end of his career as a chef. Gustavo was hooked! In 2005 he moved from hotels to nightclubs, including working at the Geha

Mega-Bar in Eilat, the busiest nightclub of the time, catering for 2,500 customers a night. In 2008 he moved back to hotel bartending and began taking on more senior roles, including event management for high-profile guests like Benjamin Netanyahu (Israel's Prime Minister). Gustavo ranks his greatest achievement to date as being part of the team that contributed towards his hotel, Herod's Vitalis Spa Resort, as being ranked as the number-one hotel in the Middle East on Trip Advisor 2017. On a personal level, Gustavo won the Eilat Bartending Competition in 2003 and 2004 and won the Barista National Competition in 2015.

FRENCH ROCK 'N' ROLL
JAMIE STEPHENSON

Jamie says: *No word of a lie, this cocktail appeared to me in a dream –*
I have no idea how the combination of ingredients manifested itself
in my subconscious, but when I made it for the first time I was blown away.
I'm so immensely proud of this drink and I love the comments
it elicits from people, especially those expecting to hate it.

30ML LA FÉE PARISIENNE ABSINTHE
20ML BRIOTTET PEACH LIQUEUR
25ML FRESH LEMON JUICE
15ML MONIN PISTACHIO SYRUP
2 DASHES ANGOSTURA BITTERS
½ EGG WHITE

METHOD: Add all the ingredients to a shaker with a large scoop of ice. Shake very well and double strain into a chilled coupette or martini glass. Garnish with a star anise.

NOTE FROM JAMIE: This drink can only be made with La Fée Parisienne Absinthe – it's quite important, not only for flavour profile but for the name itself. One of the originators of the brand was in a group called Black Box Recorder and 'French Rock 'n' Roll' was the name of one of their tracks, which fit perfectly with the idea of absinthe being the 'bad boy' of spirits.

JAMIE STEPHENSON is an absolute giant of the cocktail world. He has been a bartender for more than 20 years and has built a solid reputation as one of the best in the world. Regarded as an authority on cocktails, Jamie was described as 'Officially the best cocktail maker in the universe' by Polly Vernon in the *Observer Food Monthly*. Tom Innes, editor of *Flavour Magazine* wrote, 'He has phenomenal drinks knowledge and makes terrific cocktails'.
As the winner of five World Championship titles among countless other competitions (far too many to mention here), Jamie exudes the professionalism, passion and dedication which has led him to claim the National Bartender of the Year awards from *The Publican* Newspaper (2002), *CLASS* (2004), *THEME* (2004), *FLVR* (2004) and *Drinks International* (2006) magazines. Jamie is now committed to educating and inspiring bartenders all over the world, providing training built on many years of dedicated research and experience.

WINNER OF FLVR MAGAZINE BARTENDER OF THE YEAR COMPETITION 2004

FRENCH ROYALE

SHEKHAR GROVER

Shekhar says: *The French Royale has followed my whole Bartending Career as this cocktail was created when I took part in the Ciroc International Bartending Competition in India when I was just three months into bartending. It has a funny story behind its creation. When I was told to be ready for competition auditions the next day, I went to a lot of bars like TGI Fridays and Ruby Tuesday just to get some ideas for the competition and on cocktail presentation. At the competition, when asked by the presenter to write my ingredients on the entry form, he promptly realised where the ideas were stolen from! He therefore put pressure on me to create a new cocktail on the spot. The French Royale was created and became the best cocktail for the Northern Zone of India. Some years later, a little tweak to the recipe made me the 'Best in Cruiselines' for the World Class Global Competition*

1 SMALL BUNCH FROZEN FRESH CALIFORNIAN BLACK GRAPES, DE-SKINNED
40ML CIROC VODKA
40ML SAUTERNES DESSERT WINE
7ML CRÈME DE CASSIS
15ML FRESH LIME JUICE
7ML SIMPLE SYRUP

METHOD: Muddle 4–5 frozen de-skinned grapes in a glass shaker. Add the remaining ingredients with a scoop of ice and shake well. Double strain into a chilled martini glass. Garnish with a frozen de-skinned and cassis-infused (soak overnight) black grape or other summer fruit.

————

SHEKHAR GROVER could well be described as the greatest mixologist on water! Not to mention having the most appropriate name for a mixologist! With a career that began in 2008, he has become integral to the experience that guests encounter when travelling the world's seas on one of Royal Caribbean's stunning cruise liners. Of his many influences, Shekhar has been responsible for the implementation of new venue and menu concepts for the biggest ship in the world (at the time of writing), *Oasis of the Seas*. Indeed, his role with Royal Caribbean has seen him implement a new era of cocktails for their entire 25-ship fleet. Shekhar's victory at the 2014 *Global Travel* finals saw him come out on top of a field of 5,500 bartenders from across the world. That is some serious mixology!

WINNER OF DIAGEO WORLD CLASS GLOBAL TRAVEL 2014 (WORLD CHAMPION)

FROM SEA TO SKYE
KNEALE BROWN

Kneale says: *I wanted to create an avant garde, modern cocktail.*
Something that would twist people's perceptions of what a cocktail was,
so I removed the need for garnish, ice or textural expectations. Huge inspiration
came from a drink I had tried at the world-famous Artesian bar.
I aimed to hard filter Sea to Sky by removing all particulate matter and therefore
bind together the cocktail by subtraction rather than addition.

30ML TALISKER TEN WHISKY
80ML CABERNET SAUVIGNON VERJUS
80ML STILL MINERAL WATER
10ML 2:1 RATIO WHITE SUGAR SYRUP

METHOD: You can make one cocktail or scale up as desired. Combine all the ingredients in a mixing jug. Now pour everything through a commercial or home water filter (Brita or similar). Chill in the fridge. Serve cold in a wine glass (or tumbler) with no ice or garnish.

———————

KNEALE BROWN is British born, living in New Zealand. Nominated for the capital's Most Outstanding Bartender at the 2017 Felix Hospitality Awards, Kneale is at the cutting edge of the New Zealand mixology scene. With a career that has seen him travel widely in his quest to expand his knowledge and experience, he works hard to stay on top of developing trends and evolutions in the cocktail world. Kneale's win at the Diageo World Class event led to him placing high in the global finals, with the accolade of being the first bartender ever to mix his drink using audio (for atmosphere)!

WINNER OF DIAGEO WORLD CLASS NEW ZEALAND 2016

GIN GENIE
WAYNE COLLINS

Wayne says: *This cocktail was my first win at the Drinks International Cocktail Challenge in 2001 at Vinexpo. I'm particularly proud of this drink as at the time I was brand ambassador for Plymouth Gin. It was inspired by the Bramble cocktail of the late legend Dick Bradsell, who was someone I had worked with at a couple of venues and he was a great inspiration in my career.*

50ML GIN
6 FRESH MINT LEAVES
25ML FRESH LEMON JUICE
10ML SUGAR SYRUP
10ML SLOE GIN
10ML DAMSON GIN

METHOD: Muddle the first four ingredients together in a highball glass. Add crushed ice and 'churn'. Float the sloe and damson gins on the top and garnish with a slice of lemon, a mint sprig and a raspberry.

———————

WAYNE COLLINS is an internationally recognised, award-winning bar trainer with over 25 years of industry experience. A key figure within the bar boom of 90s London, he opened and worked at many high-profile and award-winning venues. This led to him being head hunted to become a brand ambassador and drinks stylist for various globally recognised premium spirit brands. Wayne appeared frequently on several well-known food television programmes and channels, like *Great Food Live* and Food Network, and presented the legendry Sunday cocktail slot on the BBC's hugely popular *Something for the Weekend* – a show that regularly pulled in over 1.5 million viewers. Many of Wayne's creations can be seen on drinks lists throughout the world and he has countless competition victories to his name, including Southern California Bartender of the Year 1994, Bacardi Martini Grand Prix, UK Champion 1997, and the winner of three categories at the 2005 International Cocktail Challenge at London's Excel. *The New York Times* featured Wayne as a 'British Cocktail King' and he is widely thought to have made more television appearances than any other bartender in history.

WINNER OF DRINKS INTERNATIONAL COCKTAIL CHALLENGE 2001

GORDAL NEGRONI
LAURENCE EATON

Laurence says: *Experimenting with the reaction of salt and bitter on the palate, this drink really produces a surprising outcome. Much like using citrus to balance sweetness, combining salt/saline with bitter brings out the sweeter fruity notes found in Italian bitters. This drink is an ideal introduction to the Negroni style of cocktail as the combination of bitter and salt really complements the sweeter characteristics of an Italian bitter.*

25ML TANQUERAY NO. TEN GIN
25ML MARTINI ROSSO
25ML OLIVE-STEEPED CAMPARI*

METHOD: Add all the ingredients to a mixing glass with a scoop of ice and stir until chilled. Strain into a martini glass and garnish with a Campari-Steeped Gordal Olive*.

OLIVE-STEEPED CAMPARI AND
CAMPARI-STEEPED GORDAL OLIVES*
Take 200g Gordal olives and steep in 300ml Campari for 48 hours. Strain the Campari to use in the cocktail and store the olives in a refrigerator.

LAURENCE EATON began his career in the UK as bar manager of Berry and Rye in Liverpool. It was there that he first appeared on the global cocktail radar by appearing in magazine articles and reviews. By 2016, Laurence had made his move to the Cayman Islands, bringing his considerable skills to bear on the success of The Bistro when taking on the bar manager role. That same year, having created an enormous impact by winning Diageo World Class within months of arriving, he took on the role of World Class Ambassador. Laurence is now working as a bar consultant, creating cocktail menus, recruiting and training staff, and generally putting his stamp on the Cayman Island's bar scene.

WINNER OF DIAGEO WORLD CLASS CAYMAN ISLANDS 2016

GRASS & GINGER
MUKESH PRATAP

Mukesh says: *Grass & Ginger is the best creation of my career, which I feel each time I make and serve it. This drink is very refreshing and nice to have in the afternoon. It looks like a Mojito but the taste and experience are completely different. I wish to spread more and more happiness through this amazing drink.*

5 WHITE SUGAR CUBES
1 TBSP FINELY CHOPPED FRESH GINGER
4 LIME WEDGES
2 STICKS LEMONGRASS
60ML GREY GOOSE VODKA
CLUB SODA, TO TOP UP

METHOD: Add the sugar and ginger to a highball glass and muddle. Add the lime wedges and muddle again. Cut the lemongrass into diamonds and add to the glass. Add the vodka and stir. Fill with ice and top with club soda. Garnish with a lemongrass stick (or fresh mint).

———————

MUKESH PRATAP worked at the Hyatt Regency in Delhi – from the commencement of his career in 2009 until 2014 – in a variety of departments before he discovered his love for the bar. This newfound focus led him to make the move to St Kitts, where he still works for the Nirvana restaurant. Not solely focusing on mixology, Mukesh is also an accomplished sommelier and winner of the Best Wine Service and Flair Award at the Indian Sommelier Championships 2013.

WINNER OF ST KITTS ISLAND COCKTAIL COMPETITION 2014

HELP IS ON THE WAY
TONY PEREYRA

Tony says: *I made this cocktail during the winter, and wanted to utilise ingredients that would speak for the season and that would also complement the high-proof Moonshine.*

1 EGG WHITE
15ML FRESH LEMON JUICE
45ML OLE SMOKY BLUE FLAME MOONSHINE
30ML HOLIDAY BERRY SPICED SHRUB*
20ML ROSEMARY-INFUSED VELVET FALERNUM**

METHOD: Add the egg white and lemon juice to a shaker and dry shake. Add the remaining ingredients along with a scoop of ice and shake again. Strain into a coupe glass and garnish with a lemon curd cracker, a raspberry and a mint sprig.

HOLIDAY BERRY SPICED SHRUB*
Combine 200g raspberries, 5 cloves, 1 tsp ground allspice, 5 cardamom pods and 200g sugar in a sealed container for 48 hours. Add 200ml red wine vinegar and leave for a further 48 hours, shaking occasionally. Strain the liquid and keep in a sealed container in the fridge.

ROSEMARY-INFUSED VELVET FALERNUM**
Add 6 sprigs of rosemary to 750ml falernum and allow to infuse. Leave for at least 3 days before using.

TONY PEREYRA is the co-owner and founder of the Spirits In Motion Beverage Consultancy, established in 2011. In addition, he is the bar consultant and trainer for Fleming's Prime Steakhouse and is the bar and beverage consultant for BarProducts.com, the world's largest supplier of bar equipment. Tony spends much of his time advising on and directing the opening of numerous branded restaurant chains, most notably being responsible for the opening of the Jack Nicklaus Golden Bear Grills in Charleston and Fort Lauderdale. Tony is a highly skilled and respected mixologist and his win at the Ole Smoky Masters of Moonshine competition in 2015 marked the inaugural staging of this annual event.

HITTING LOCH BOTTOM
ALISTAIR REYNOLDS

Alistair says: *My inspiration for this drink lies in celebrations.*
A good dram can be mixed with the king of drinks for celebrating... Champagne.
Plus, the notes I find in Blue Label, Earl Grey tea, smoke, apple and biscuits
are all highlighted by the ingredients I chose.

40ML JOHNNIE WALKER BLUE LABEL WHISKY
15ML BERGAMOT PURÉE*
25ML BLUSH CIDER
2 DASHES FERNET-BRANCA
RUINART BLANC DE BLANC CHAMPAGNE, TO TOP UP

METHOD: Add all the ingredients except the Champagne to a shaker with a scoop of ice and shake well. Strain into a sherry glass and top up with the Champagne.

BERGAMOT PURÉE*
Brew 100ml Earl Grey tea using 1 tsp loose tea. Now combine with 100g caster sugar and stir until the sugar has dissolved. Allow to cool.

NOTE FROM ALI: *I presented this drink by setting the glass bottom into a concrete cylinder and freezing onto a silver tray. A hammer is used to break the ice and release the drink.*

———————

ALISTAIR REYNOLDS describes himself as an individual that is inspired by the food and drink industry. Over a period of more than ten years he has built an international reputation for excellence. He has played a direct role in establishing global recognition for the venues he has worked with, including the Michelin-starred Pollen Street Social, and gaining the Tales of the Cocktail, Best International Cocktail Bar award for the Hawksmoor, London. Alistair won the Glenfiddich Malt Mastermind in 2015, and became the Diageo Bartender of the Year and the Imbibe Bar Personality of the Year, both in 2016. He currently works as the Diageo Luxury Portfolio Ambassador for the UK and Europe.

WINNER OF DIAGEO WORLD CLASS GB 2015

IT WAS ALL A DREAM
DARNELL HOLGUIN

Darnell says: *My cocktail was inspired by a traditional Dominican breakfast drink called Morir Soñando. It consists of orange juice, evaporated milk and sugar. My mother would make that for my brother and I every morning for breakfast. The amaro and spice resemble another traditional Dominican drink called Mama Juana. I wanted to put all of my culture into that cocktail.*

45ML BACARDI OCHO RUM
45ML PASSION FRUIT CONDENSED MILK*
60ML ORANGE JUICE
10ML AVERNA AMARO
7ML ST. ELIZABETH ALLSPICE DRAM OR PIMENTO DRAM

METHOD: Add all the ingredients to a shaker with a scoop of ice and shake well. Strain into a tin cup. Fill with crushed ice. Garnish with an orange slice and a mint sprig.

PASSION FRUIT CONDENSED MILK*
Combine 300ml passion fruit purée, 300g granulated sugar and 200ml evaporated milk. Either shake together in a container or use a blender for ease.

———————

DARNELL HOLGUIN is an industry veteran from New York City, having worked over 11 years in the cocktail business. He has worked in a wide range of prominent bars and restaurants in NYC, such as Donatella restaurant, and with key brands such as Bathtub Gin. He currently runs the bar programme at Fifty Restaurant in the West Village. In 2015, Darnell was voted as one of the top ten bartenders in New York City by *Time Out* magazine, and in 2017 he became the East Coast regional champion at the Bacardi Legacy competition.

WINNER OF BACARDI LEGACY EAST COAST 2017

JIRO DREAMS OF MARTINI
MATEUSZ SZUCHNIK

Mateusz says: *I created this cocktail, inspired by a Japanese chef and owner of Sukiyabashi Jiro, the very famous Jiro Ono. His craft and innovative methods used in modern sushi preparation pushed me to redefine this vision of the classic gin martini.*

50ML TANQUERAY No. TEN GIN
15ML BERGAMOT-INFUSED CHOYA PLUM WINE*
2 DASHES RICE VINEGAR

METHOD: Add all the ingredients to a mixing glass with a scoop of ice and stir. Strain into a chilled coupette glass and garnish with a drop of Grapefruit Olive Oil**.

BERGAMOT-INFUSED CHOYA PLUM WINE*
Combine 100g caster sugar with 2 drops natural bergamot oil and 700ml Choya wine. Stir until the sugar has completely dissolved.

GRAPEFRUIT OLIVE OIL**
Combine the zest from 3 pink grapefruits with 300ml olive oil and sous vide for 3 hours at 45°C. Alternatively leave to stand for 24 hours. Strain and store in a sealed bottle.

MATEUSZ SZUCHNIK has been bartending since 2009 and is the owner of El Koktel in Warsaw, Poland, winner of the Best Cocktail Bar of 2015, Poland. In addition to living and working in Poland, Mateusz spent a couple of years in London working at the Michelin-starred Pollen Street Social and the iconic LAB Bar. Mateusz is the winner of Bols Around the World, Poland 2013, Tahnona Society 2016, Wild Turkey Bourbon Cocktail Competition 2016 and the Coffee in Good Spirits National Cocktail Competition 2017. In addition to competing, Mateusz is also in demand for his knowledge and skills. He has been a judge at the 2014 Polish Bols competition and the Czech Diageo World Class competition. He has also delivered master-classes at the Ristor Expo in Italy and Bar Convent in Berlin.

JOURNEY
ABHIJIT ROY

Abhijit says: *The inspiration for the cocktail came from my mum.*
She always said that if you want to become a good person, then you should respect
all you meet. And if you want to become a successful man you should work hard.
My journey began in a small hotel and hard work has taken me to the Hilton.
I have made a few cocktails on my journey but I love this cocktail so much.

LAGAVULIN SINGLE MALT WHISKY, FOR 'MISTING'
45ML BOMBAY SAPPHIRE GIN
30ML ORANGE JUICE
15ML GREEN APPLE SYRUP
10ML FRESH LIME JUICE

METHOD: Prepare a goblet by spraying with a fine mist of Lagavulin Single Malt Whisky. Add all the ingredients to a shaker with a scoop of ice, shake for 5–10 seconds. Strain into the prepared goblet and garnish with a sprig of fresh rosemary.

———————

ABHIJIT ROY's dream was always to become a bartender. Coming from a poor background his goal was always to work in the food and beverage industry and make his mark by creating and developing drinks that would leave a lasting impression on his guests and customers. He has worked in numerous top-end hotel bars, the highlights of which are the Park Plaza Hotel and the Bangalore Hilton, the venue at which his award-winning cocktail was created. Abhijit has certainly managed to turn his dream into a reality, as is reflected by the countless mentions he receives on Trip Advisor and the Hilton guest satisfaction webpage (where you can read more about him). His drink, Journey, was his first victory in a major cocktail competition and illustrates his flair for creative mixology.

KAYANUSA
OSMUND BERNARD

෴

Osmund says: *During the Diageo competition, my hometown was celebrating its harvest festival, called 'Kaamatan and Gawai', so this drink is dedicated to the celebration that occurred while I was away from my country competing. I also wanted to introduce these new flavours and my local ingredients to a global audience.*

60ML KETEL ONE VODKA
1 BSP KAYA JAM
1 BSP COCONUT PURÉE
10ML SOTO SYRUP*
15ML KALAMANSI JUICE

METHOD: Add all the ingredients to a shaker with a scoop of ice and shake well. Strain into an ice-filled old-fashioned glass and garnish with a mint sprig, lime and a pandan leaf.

SOTO SYRUP*
Heat 1 litre water with 1kg sugar and stir until dissolved. Now add the below ingredients: 40g lemongrass, 40g galangal, 40g ginger, 10g garlic, 10g shallot, 15g cinnamon, 5g star anise, 2g cardamom pods, 1g cloves, 10g candlenut, 1 tsp chicken stock powder. Simmer for 10 minutes. Allow to cool, then rest in the fridge for 24 hours. After 24 hours strain into a bottle and keep refrigerated.

OSMUND BERNARD has been working as a bartender in Kuala Lumpur, Malaysia since 2009. Responsible for opening the bars at Tujo and IKKI, he is also one of Malaysia's top bartender trainers. Osmund's first competitive success came when he was runner-up in the 2012 Malaysian Iron Bartender Competition. In the same year, he went a stage further in the Bols Around the World competition, becoming the Malaysian national champion. In 2013 Osmund added to his achievements when he won the Luna Bagus International Cocktail Open. Two years later, at his first attempt, he was the runner-up at the Diageo World Class, Malaysia championships, the competition he went on to win in 2016.

LA CATRINA

PHILIPP M. ERNST

Philipp says: *My inspiration for this cocktail was the words of Max La Rocca: 'Keep it simple, far away from the moon'. So I created a well-balanced drink that would be easy produce in a 'real bar setting'. The guests in my bar love the show with smoke! So, you have a simple drink, well balanced with a new taste, easy to handle and a great show for your guests!*

50ML DON JULIO AÑEJO TEQUILA
10ML RUNNY HONEY
5ML JÄGERMEISTER
2 DASHES THE BITTER TRUTH CHOCOLATE BITTERS
2 DASHES FEE BROTHERS ORANGE BITTERS

METHOD: Stir all ingredients together in a mixing glass with a scoop of ice. Strain the cocktail into a tumbler with a large (5cm x 5cm) ice cube. Place the glass in a glass dome and smoke the drink with hickory wood using a smoking gun.

————

PHILIPP ERNST is the owner of Josef Cocktail Bar in Vienna and More Than Cocktails, a training and events company. With a background in 5-star hotels, Phillip has been a leading figure in the Austrian bartending scene since 1998.

He often delivers presentations to the global cocktail community at international exhibitions and shows, as well as featuring as a guest trainer at major training academies like the Beefeater London Gin school, the Austrian Bartender School and the World Class Boot Camp in Madrid. As a guest bartender, Philipp is in great demand and regularly travels to Salzburg, Vienna, Munich, Berlin and Stuttgart to wow audiences with his bartending skills. Philipp is also an IBA-registered Master of Bartending, Wine and Spirits.

LA FLORA
PONGPAK SUDTHIPONGSE

❧

Pongpak says: *My cocktail was inspired by two prohibition gin cocktails: the Bee's Knees and White Lady. I wanted to create a cocktail that is unique, but also easy to replicate and maintain consistency, while also playing with all the senses of the drinker. I created two textures: the sweet and floral lotus on egg foam, then the cocktail that follows. The lingering floral notes kick into the nose and keep reminding the drinker to take the next sip.*

45ML GIN
10ML COINTREAU
10ML ST GERMAIN ELDERFLOWER LIQUEUR
10ML LOTUS NECTAR*
20ML FRESH LEMON JUICE
15ML EGG WHITE
1 DASH TONIC BITTERS

METHOD: Add all the ingredients to a shaker and dry shake. Then add a scoop of ice and shake again. Double strain into a coupe glass and garnish with an edible flower, thyme and lemon peel.

LOTUS NECTAR*
Mix together 1 part natural lotus syrup, 2 parts honey and 1 part water.

———————

PONGPAK SUDTHIPONGSE is co-owner of the Villa di Sorrento Restaurant and Bar and former partner and beverage director at the Why97 pub and restaurant, both in Bangkok. His hospitality career begun in 2009 subsequent to achieving an MBA in investment banking, and since 2015 he has worked as a consultant and trainer for bars and bartenders. In 2014 he entered the Diageo World Class event, his first competition, where he achieved the runner-up position along with winning the South East Asia Flavour Challenge. The following year, Pongpak became champion at the same event and then went on to represent Thailand in the global finals where he placed in the world's top 20. His position as one of Thailand's finest mixologists has led to his involvement in the judging of numerous top-level cocktail competitions. Pongpak still works as an investment banker during the day and follows his passion for mixology by working behind the bar in the evening.

56

LA VIE ROSE 75
ALLISON ISAMBERT

Allison says: *The inspiration for this cocktail was the love story of me and my husband. He swept me off my feet and 'La Vie en Rose' played at our wedding. We met when he worked at a restaurant in Laguna Beach called French 75. I combined the two names with an updated version of a Rose cocktail – the bridge between France and America. The infusion of the roses makes it aromatic while the cardamom added a little passion to the palate.*

45ML SILVER DRY GIN
15ML FRESH LIME JUICE
15ML ROSE WATER CARDAMOM SIMPLE SYRUP*
2 DROPS PEYCHAUD'S BITTERS
ROSÉ CHAMPAGNE, TO TOP UP

METHOD: Combine the first four ingredients in a mixing glass with a scoop of ice. Stir and strain into a coupe glass which has been rimmed with a pinch of muddled candied rose petals**.
Top up with rosé Champagne.

ROSE WATER CARDAMOM SIMPLE SYRUP*
Combine 100g caster sugar and 240ml rose water in a small saucepan, simmering and stirring until the sugar is dissolved. Add 4 tbsp of cardamom and continue to simmer on low heat for 5 minutes. Let cool, then refrigerate and allow to steep for up to 3 days. Strain to remove solids.

MUDDLED DRIED CANDIED ROSE PETALS**
Rinse and pat dry rose petals. Paint both sides of petals with simple syrup, egg whites or prepared meringue powder, then sprinkle with caster sugar. Dry on parchment or wax paper overnight. After completely dry, crumble.

ALLISON ISAMBERT has been plying her trade as a bartender/mixologist on the Californian bar scene since 2000. In that time she has dedicated herself to the development of her craft and the creation of some of the finest cocktails the USA has to offer. Her skills are in great demand and as a consequence she has divided her time between a variety of diverse projects. She has bartended for Renaissance Entertainment Productions, was the head banquet bartender for Montage 5-Star Resort and is currently events bartender for 100Eats Events. In addition to her mixology skills, Allison is also a certified sommelier and since 2015 has also worked as a sommelier tour guide in Napa/Sonoma, California.

WINNER OF NOLET'S COCKTAIL COMPETITION 2015

57

LATIN QUARTER
BOUDY GHOSTINE

Boudy says: *This drink is inspired by the popular casual drink Cuba Libre and the elegant Daiquiri cocktail. All the ingredients in the cocktail have a connection or a bond with the Latin culture. The rum was originally produced in Cuba (now in Puerto Rico), Coca-Cola came to Cuba around 1900, and finally the Spanish PX Sherry is a tribute to Don Facundo Bacardi Massó (the creator of Bacardi rum) who started out as a wine merchant.*

30ml Bacardi Carta Blanca Rum
30ml Bacardi Gold Rum
25–30ml fresh lime juice
25ml cola syrup
1 bsp Pedro Ximenez Sherry
10ml egg white

METHOD: Add all the ingredients except the egg white to a Boston (2-part) shaker with a scoop of ice. Shake hard to mix and chill. Double strain the drink into a spare glass or jug and keep to the side. Discard all the ice from the shaker and now add the egg white. Return the shaken drink to the shaker along with the egg white and shake hard again. By shaking again with no ice, the egg white will transform to a lovely thick foam. Finally, pour the drink in to a coupette glass and garnish with a maraschino sherry dipped in pop rock sugar (popping candy).

NOTE FROM PAUL: *Boudy recommends a technique called the reverse dry shake. This enables him to create a thick foam on the head of the drink. I recommend following the technique closely for optimum results.*

BOUDY GHOSTINE is a major character on the Swedish cocktail scene. He is a former brand ambassador for the Swedish Cocktail Boutique as well as being the bar and beverage consultant for The Spirit Syndicate in Bangkok. Over the last decade, he has managed several highly acclaimed cocktail bars in Stockholm, which has also provided him with the opportunity to showcase his mixing skills at the world's biggest competitions. In 2011, he became the Diageo World Class Swedish bartender of the year and represented Sweden in the global finals held in New Delhi. And two years later went on to achieve even greater heights by finishing second in the world with the recipe he has contributed to this book.

LEGEND REVIVER
WADE CLEOPHAS

Wade says: *When I think of rum, the first things that come to mind are travelling and exotic places. It's so fitting that I actually work on a cruise ship. So, I decided to merge two exceptionally good classics, the Manhattan and the Sazerac, using only certain elements from each, creating something that is just as good with Bacardi Ocho. The name comes from back in the day when folks used to tell stories beginning, 'As Legend has it...' Hence the name Legend Reviver.*

A MIST OF ABSINTHE
50ML BACARDI OCHO RUM
20ML STAR ANISE-INFUSED SWEET VERMOUTH*
8ML CARAMEL–CINNAMON SYRUP**
3 DROPS FEE BROTHERS WHISKEY BARREL AGED BITTERS

METHOD: Begin by spraying a martini glass with a mist of absinthe and set aside. Add all the remaining ingredients to a mixing glass with a large scoop of ice (it should fill 70% of the mixing glass). Stir well and strain into the prepared martini glass. Garnish with 'iconic' designed lemon peel and star anise (see photograph).

STAR ANISE-INFUSED SWEET VERMOUTH*
Add 12 star anise pods to 1 bottle of sweet vermouth and leave to infuse for 8 hours. Remove the star anise and retain the vermouth in a sealed bottle.

CARAMEL–CINNAMON SYRUP**
Combine 2 parts Monin caramel syrup with 1 part Monin cinnamon syrup.

WADE CLEOPHAS is from Cape Town in South Africa and is another of our super-talented water-based bartenders. Starting in 2005, Wade worked around the globe but always had one goal in mind – to work on the cruise liners. It took him five years of rejected applications before he eventually landed his dream job with Norwegian Cruises. Unlike most bartenders, the great cruise-based bartenders don't have the same opportunities to showcase their skills in competitions, namely because they are hardly ever in one place. However, Wade grasped the chance to enter the Bacardi Legacy Cruise Liner Competition and his subsequent victory clearly establishes him as one of the world's best. I wonder if any of the companies that rejected him are reading this?

WINNER OF BACARDI LEGACY GLOBAL CRUISE LINER COMPETITION 2017

LOVE LETTER
JOÃO RODRIGUES

João says: *I have a lot of tourists who visit the Columbus bar to write postcards to their families. I was inspired to create a cocktail that provided a postcard with the cocktail so that they can drink and write together. The cocktail should be served with the card, a silver pen and (if possible) edible ink.*

50ML RON DE ZACAPA 23 RUM
30ML STOUT REDUCTION*
10ML CHARCOAL SYRUP**
OLD TOBACCO SMOKE***, TO TOP

METHOD: Place all the ingredients in a shaker with a scoop of ice and shake. Strain into a pipe-shaped glass (or old-fashioned tumbler) and add the Old Tobacco Smoke to the top with the syringe.

STOUT REDUCTION*
Take 1 bottle of stout beer (João used a Portuguese beer called Maldita Russian Standard) and boil until it is reduced by half. Allow to cool, then refrigerate.

CHARCOAL SYRUP**
Infuse 20 charcoal pills in 250ml water for 2 days. Add 250g sugar and warm until the sugar is fully dissolved. Allow to cool, then refrigerate.

OLD TOBACCO SMOKE***
João used a syringe to extract the vapor from an e-cigarette. He used nicotine-free e-liquid and chose 'old tobacco' flavour for this drink.

JOÃO RODRIGUES' bartending career started in the Columbus Cocktail and Wine Bar in Faro, Portugal, initially to pay for his university education in hotel management. However, he fell in love with the cocktail art form and decided to follow his passion for bartending. Nowadays, he is the head bartender at Columbus, where he and his team members have won several awards including the Best Bar Team and Best Bar Menu at the 2014 Lisbon Bar Show. João also won Best Cocktail at the 2014 Melius Magellan competition and went one step further in 2015 when he became overall champion. His victory in the 2016 Portuguese Diageo World Class event has led to him being featured in top magazines like GQ and appearing in brand video advertisements.

WINNER OF DIAGEO WORLD CLASS PORTUGAL 2016

MADAM LILY
NOAM SHARET

Noam says: Growing up in a small village in the north of Israel,
I always felt connected to nature. Therefore, while starting to create my legacy cocktail
I was immediately attracted to the nature of Cuba. I discovered the white mariposa –
the national flower of Cuba, and that was the inspiration for my cocktail.
I was trying to create a cocktail that would have an amazing aroma,
just like the flower which is known for its special fragrance.

3–4 SLICES OF GRANNY SMITH APPLE (ABOUT ¼ OF AN APPLE)
22.5ML SUGAR SYRUP
22.5ML FRESH LIME JUICE
22.5ML CALVADOS
45ML BACARDI CARTA BLANCA RUM
ABSINTHE, FOR RINSING

METHOD: Muddle the apple with the sugar syrup in the shaker, then add the lime juice, calvados and Bacardi. Spray absinthe into a chilled Champagne glass. Add a scoop of ice to the shaker and shake well. Double strain the cocktail into the absinthe-rinsed glass. Garnish with a twist of lime and an edible white flower.

———

NOAM SHARET began her bartending career with formal cocktail training on the Zman Amiti Mixing with the Best cocktail course and the Pernod Ricard BarSmarts course. In 2013 she started working as a waitress at the Valley Bar in Ein Harod before progressing to the role of bartender in 2015 at Mashya in Tel Aviv. Stints at Double Standard and A23 followed before taking on her first head bartender role at the Guest Room. Noam's 2017 Bacardi Legacy win led to her representing Israel in the global finals, where she reached the top 16 in the world. As a result of her win and her fabulous award-winning cocktail, she has been invited to appear as a guest bartender for many shifts around the world, including at Theory in Athens and Door 74 in Amsterdam. Noam also runs regular cocktail presentations and masterclasses.

MADAME Y PATRÓN

ANDREA MELIS

Andrea says: *My inspiration was to create a drink that envisioned an ideal love story: the classic touch of the Champagne cocktail, paired with the bold agave notes of Patrón Añejo tequila. Working with all the flavour characteristics imbued in both sublime liquids, a perfect pairing was born – introducing Madame y Patrón.*

35ML PATRÓN AÑEJO TEQUILA
20ML OLOROSO SHERRY
20ML AGAVE CARAMEL
6 DROPS OF XOCOLATL MOLE BITTERS
CHAMPAGNE, TO TOP UP

METHOD: Add all ingredients, including the Champagne, to a mixing glass full of ice and stir. Strain into a Champagne saucer and top with additional Champagne if required.

———

ANDREA MELIS was born in Sardinia in the 1980s. His first cocktail bartending job came at the age of 18 in Italy while attending university. After graduating, he decided to use his bartending skills as a means to fund his travelling, and subsequent to a short period in Spain, ended up in London in 2012. His first job in the city was right back at the bottom of the bartending ladder, as a bar-back. However, there was no denying Andrea's skills and over the following few years he rose through the ranks to tend bar at the Blind Pig at the Social Eating House (named World's Best Restaurant Bar in 2014) and then go on to become the head bartender at the Blue Bar at The Berkeley. Andrea has entered a variety of cocktail competitions 'for fun' during his time in the UK, with his Patrón Perfectionist victory being the highlight so far.

WINNER OF PATRÓN PERFECTIONIST COCKTAIL COMPETITION, LONDON 2017

MAGNUS
KENNEDY NASCIMENTO

Kennedy says: *This cocktail is inspired by a chef that I worked with called Magnus. He pays very deep attention to the ingredients he uses in the kitchen and has been a big influence on the approach I take to bartending.*

45ML TANQUERAY NO. TEN GIN
30ML NOILLY PRAT VERMOUTH
30ML CYNAR LIQUEUR
2 DROPS SALT SOLUTION*

METHOD: Add all the ingredients to a mixing glass with a scoop of ice and stir until nicely chilled. Strain into a small coupette glass and garnish with some lime peel and an Amarena (sour) cherry.

SALT SOLUTION*
Dissolve 15g salt in 100ml of water.

————————

KENNEDY NASCIMENTO is a young Brazilian bartender with a lot of high-level experience. He has worked as head bartender for the Vegas Group and as a lecturer for the ABS (Association of Brazilian Sommeliers). In addition to winning Diageo World Class Brazil, Kennedy also won the wider Latin America competition and is also the winner of the Bols Around the World Latin American cocktail competition. He has also won numerous Brazilian National cocktail competitions. Kennedy is now (as we go to print) preparing to open his own bar.

WINNER OF DIAGEO WORLD CLASS BRAZIL 2015

MARIEL
KENTARO SATOH

Kentaro says: *The Cuban port city Mariel is gaining attention globally for its growing international trade and is becoming Cuba's window to the rest of the world. More than 200 years ago, Japan also went through a similar transformation. In 1859, Yokohama was the first port city to start trading with other countries. My legacy cocktail Mariel, aims to bridge these two cultures and create a new 'port city cocktail'.*

40ML BACARDI OCHO RUM
20ML FRESH ORANGE JUICE
15ML COCONUT WATER
10ML HONEY
2 DASHES ABSINTHE

METHOD: Add all the ingredients to a cocktail shaker with a scoop of ice and shake well. Double strain into a martini glass and garnish with a sprinkling of ground cinnamon.

———————

KENTARO SATOH is the owner of BAR Day Cocktail in Yokohama, Japan, which opened in 2008. Here he focuses on the creation of cocktails using homemade spirits and liqueurs and employing the latest and most popular techniques from around the world. In 2010, Kentaro received the Grand Prix Yokohama Mayor Prize at the Yokohama Cocktail Competition, a highly regarded award, and in 2011 he was invited to become the vodka ambassador for the Absolut Academy in Sweden. In 2012 he won a number of cocktail competitions culminating in becoming the champion at the Alegría de Mexico Tequila Cocktail Grand Prix.

MARSHALL
DAVIDE BONCIMINO

Davide says: *The Marshall is created and named in honour and tribute to a regular customer: Chris Marshall. He is passionate about rum and good drinks. A supporter of both bars and bartenders, he is now considered a bar influencer. His passion and values inspire people, bringing them together. Whichever country you work in, every bar and bartender has a 'Marshall', that customer who is passionate and inspiring – and always with a story to tell.*

I BSP BLACK PEPPERCORNS
40ML BACARDI OCHO RUM
15ML LUSTAU DRY OLOROSO DON NUÑO SHERRY
10ML ST GERMAIN ELDERFLOWER LIQUEUR
20ML FRESH LEMON JUICE
7.5ML RE'AL BLUE AGAVE NECTAR

METHOD: Muddle the black peppercorns in the shaker, then add all the remaining ingredients. Shake hard and double strain into a coupe glass. Garnish with lemon peel.

————————

DAVIDE BONCIMINO's career as a bartender began in Biella, a small city in the north of Italy. Davide moved from his hometown to Milan to expand his knowledge and after a couple of months, made the big step of moving to London in December 2013. In September 2014, he joined Mr Fogg's Residence, one of the most renowned Mayfair cocktail bars and named as one of the 100 Best Bars in the World in 2015. In the same year, he took part in 13 contests, winning various regional events and moving on to UK national finals with brands such as Russian Standard and Gin No. 209. He also entered Bacardi Legacy and Diageo World Class competitions before winning the UK title for Don Papa rum. That victory led to him being invited to run cocktail masterclasses in the Philippines and Singapore and eventually, in 2016, move to the latter permanently. Since that move, he has opened the Lime House Caribbean cocktail bar and run The Other Room, a highly innovative cocktail haven.

WINNER OF BACARDI LEGACY SINGAPORE 2017

MEMENTO
MARTIN BORNEMANN

Martin says: *A Memento cocktail not only represents looking back but also having something to idolise. This idol could be a musician or the cantineros who brought us legendary cocktails such as the Daiquiri and the Mojito, or it could be the Bacardi family who rose up twice and led us into the 'New Golden Age of Cocktails'. My cocktail brings back the iconic Bacardi Banana Daiquiri with a new twist, in a modern, fruity yet dry and well-balanced way.*

2CM PIECE OF BANANA
30ML FRESH LIME JUICE
50ML BACARDI CARTA BLANCA RUM
15ML CHARTREUSE YELLOW LIQUEUR
20ML SALTED PEANUT BUTTER SYRUP*
2 DASHES PEYCHAUD'S BITTERS

METHOD: In a shaker, muddle the banana together with the lime juice, then add all the other ingredients. Fill the shaker with ice cubes and give it a good shake. Double strain into a chilled coupette or flute glass. Garnish with a banana leaf.

SALTED PEANUT BUTTER SYRUP*
To a bottle of Monin Peanut Butter Syrup, add 2 heaped tbsp fine sea salt and shake well until the salt has dissolved.

ALTERNATIVE RECIPE FOR
HOMEMADE PEANUT BUTTER SYRUP
For 1 litre, dissolve 500g sugar in 500ml water and bring to the boil whilst stirring, then take off the heat and stir in about 350g of creamy peanut butter and 2 tbsp fine sea salt. Transfer to a tall container and put in fridge for a minimum of 6 hours. Hold back the fat that sits on top and pour out the Peanut Butter Syrup.

MARTIN BORNEMANN has been bartending since 2007 when he graduated from Barschule Rostock in Germany. Since then he has spent the entirety of his bartending career in Switzerland, progressing from his first full-time job as a bartender at the 5-star Victoria–Jungfrau Grand Hotel and Spa to becoming the bar manager there just three years later. After running a variety of other establishments over the following four years, Martin opened Werk8 in Basel, where he was responsible for the design and development of a new bar concept for Switzerland, housed in a disused fabric hall. In 2017 Martin entered his first ever cocktail contest, the Bacardi Legacy Switzerland competition, where he became the national champion at his first attempt. Thereafter he represented his country in the global finals, reaching the top 16 out of 38 national champions.

WINNER OF BACARDI LEGACY SWITZERLAND 2017

66

MEN'S TALK
JACKO CHANG

Jacko says: *The inspiration for my drink comes from when men get together.*
Some smoke cigars, some have cigarettes (so I express this image by using cinnamon to
smoke the glass), and they talk about everything without rules and without worries.
In my opinion, this kind of moment is one of the best that men have!
I wanted to memorise this wonderful moment through this cocktail.

45ML DON JULIO REPOSADO TEQUILA
15ML TALISKER TEN WHISKY
15ML CARPANO ANTICA FORMULA VERMOUTH
15ML APEROL
5ML FRANGELICO
A CINNAMON STICK, FOR SMOKING

METHOD: Add all the ingredients except the cinnamon to a mixing glass with a scoop of ice and stir. Take a brandy snifter glass, set light to a cinnamon stick and smoke the glass by circulating the smouldering stick inside of it. Now strain the cocktail into the glass and garnish with some grated chocolate.

————

JACKO CHANG is a Taiwanese bartender with more than a decade of experience working in some of the most respected establishments in Asia. Starting as a bartender at the On Tap Sports Bar in 2007, he progressed to become the head bartender at the Mandarin Oriental in Taipei and the general manager and head bartender at the Don Quixote Bar in Nanjing. In addition to his bartending role, he also works as a voice for the industry, providing guest lectures on mixology and hospitality at the National Taiwan University and the Fu Jen Catholic University. Jacko's triumph in the 2015 Diageo World Class event led to him representing his country in the global championship.

MEZCALITA

TED DAKO

Ted says: *Trader Vic's Mai Tai is my favourite cocktail, and tequila and mezcal are my favourite spirits, so I made a Mexican twist on the Mai Tai and named it the Mezcalita. The Angostura float will slowly disappear every time you take a sip, which will change the flavour profile of the drink over time. The burning rosemary sprig gives a nice aroma that represents a Mexican market.*

20ML VIDA MEZCAL
30ML OCHO BLANCO TEQUILA
30ML FRESH LIME JUICE
30ML ORGEAT SYRUP
ANGOSTURA BITTERS, FOR THE FLOAT

METHOD: Add the first four ingredients to a shaker with a scoop of ice and shake well. Double strain into a double old-fashioned glass over a large chunk of ice. Float a layer of Angostura bitters on the surface and garnish with a burning rosemary sprig.

———————

TED DAKO is the owner of We Got Spirit Cocktail Catering and Dako Consulting, two companies that between them provide high-level cocktail bartender services, training and advice for the Danish hospitality industry. Prior to launching his companies, Ted worked as a bartender and mixologist in France, Sweden and Denmark. It is clear that his skills impacted the success of the bars he worked with, as two of them won the Copenhagen's Best Bar award during his tenure – Bar25 in 2015 and Curfew in 2017. After winning the Diageo World Class for Denmark in 2015, Ted won the Danish Cocktail Championships in 2016 and went on to place fourth in the World Cocktail Championship in Tokyo.

NACHO LIBRE
ELAD BARUCH

Elad says: *I stumbled upon an old recipe from my great-great grandfather for a hot and spicy homemade oil. Although I disliked it as a child, I eventually fell in love with the taste and texture. I wanted to incorporate it in one of my cocktails and show the world that there is good to be found in anything – eventually. The name was inspired by Jack Black's character in the movie* Nacho Libre. *It has a spicy kick to it just like the ones Nacho experiences wrestling.*

60ML DON JULIO BLANCO TEQUILA
40ML FRESH LIME JUICE
20ML AGAVE SYRUP
7.5ML CHARTREUSE LIQUEUR
15ML PIERRE FERRAND DRY CURAÇAO
5 DROPS HOMEMADE CHILLI OIL*

METHOD: Begin by preparing your coupe glass by adding a rim of Chilli and Atlantic Sea Salt Mix**. Now combine all the cocktail ingredients in the shaker with a scoop of ice and shake vigorously. Fine strain into the prepared coupe glass.

HOMEMADE CHILLI OIL*
Cut 3 medium-sized fresh chilli peppers (choose a variety depending upon heat level required) into thin slivers. Combine 1 litre top-quality olive oil and the chilli slivers in a glass jar and let sit for 2-3 days in a cool place (about 25°C).

CHILLI AND ATLANTIC SEA SALT MIX**
Mix 1 bsp Atlantic sea salt with ¼ bsp of chilli powder. Muddle until the mix is consistent and unified.

———————

ELAD BARUCH is one of the biggest names on the Israeli bartending scene. His career began in 2009 when he joined the respected Imagine Bar Services company in Tel Aviv. His talents came to the surface rapidly as he rose to the position of beverage director within just one year. By 2013, Elad's cocktail bartending skills had become apparent at a national level and he was given a place in the Israeli national team to compete in the Ketel One Bartending League in Amsterdam. The current peak of his competitive career was winning the Diageo World Class Israel competition in 2016, which prompted him to launch his own worldwide training consultancy DKC in 2017.

NAUGHTY CHRISTINE

AKASH TOMAR

Akash says: *This cocktail is inspired by a European couple who came to my bar and asked me to fix my choice of cocktail. The gentleman then asked me if I could fix a drink to make his wife 'naughty tonight'! I created this drink and upon discovering his wife's name was Christine, decided to call it Naughty Christine.*

40ML OBAN SINGLE MALT WHISKY

6 X 1CM CUBES FRESH APPLE

20ML GRAND MARNIER

30ML CINNAMON SYRUP

METHOD: Muddle the apples in a shaker with a little Oban. Add the remaining ingredients and a scoop of ice, then shake. Strain into an ice-filled rocks glass and garnish with some Oban-poached apple pieces and some cinnamon chocolates.

———————

AKASH TOMAR is from Lucknow, Uttar Pradesh in India. Throughout his career he has worked predominantly in India with one year in Kenya. He is a dedicated professional who is always seeking to improve his skills, and accordingly has passed his professional mixology training but still attends as many additional training programmes and workshops as he is able. Likewise, as a keen traveller, he takes every opportunity to visit top bars where he can pick the brains of the finest mixologists around. This dedication to self-improvement has resulted in an impressive list of competition victories, including the Bacardi Martini Grand Prix in Goa 2009, the Ambrosia Indspirit competition 2009 and the Diageo World Class 2015, Kenya. As a result, he was also invited to join the judging panel for the 2016 staging of this competition.

WINNER OF DIAGEO WORLD CLASS KENYA 2015

NEGRONI DEL PROFESSORE
MATTIA PASTORI

Mattia says: *My drink is inspired by a guest that usually drank a Boulevardier cocktail. After two cocktails he decided to smoke a Toscanello Italian cigar aromatised with coffee. I wanted to try and recreate the same combination of experiences in my drink.*

30ML WILD TURKEY RYE WHISKEY
30ML CAMPARI
30ML CINZANO 1757 VERMOUTH ROSSO
COFFEE BEANS, FOR SMOKING

METHOD: Add all the ingredients to a mixing glass with a scoop of ice and stir. Strain into an old-fashioned glass over an 'ice ball' or a large ice cube. Smoke with coffee beans.

————————

MATTIA PASTORI has been plying his trade as a top-class mixologist since the turn of the century! Firstly, working in regional Italian bars and then progressing to head the bar teams at some of the most recognisable hotels in the world, including Milan's Park Hyatt, Armani Hotel and the Mandarin Bar at the Mandarin Oriental. In 2009, Mattia won the Aibes National Caribbean Cocktail Competition. In 2011 he became a finalist at his first attempt at Diageo World Class Italy, followed closely by reaching the final of Bacardi Legacy Italy in 2012. At his second attempt, Mattia won Diageo World Class Italy 2013 and went on to finish tenth in the global finals the same year. This was the first of his two World Class titles. Mattia has now turned his attention back to the family hospitality business, an Italian cafeteria and gelateria.

WINNER OF DIAGEO WORLD CLASS ITALY 2016

NIGHT QUEEN

AYIP DZUHRI

Ayip says: *My inspiration came from the Night Queen, a magical flower from the central region of Indonesia, specifically in Central Java. The flower only blooms at night and is believed to be a symbol of prosperity and warm unconditional love. That's why this flower is always worn by the groom during traditional wedding ceremonies.*

50ML KETEL ONE VODKA
10ML MANCINO VERMOUTH BIANCO
10ML ST. GERMAIN ELDERFLOWER LIQUEUR
10ML LEMONGRASS SYRUP
15ML FRESH LEMON JUICE
3 DASHES NIGHT QUEEN TINCTURE*

METHOD: Add all the ingredients to a shaker with a scoop of ice. Shake vigorously and double strain into a coupette glass. Garnish with a Night Queen flower.

NIGHT QUEEN TINCTURE*
Combine 100g Night Queen flower petals, 10g lemon peel and 200ml food-grade 96% alcohol. Cook sous vide at 50ºC for 45 minutes, then strain. Allow to cool, then keep in an airtight container.

———

AYIP DZUHRI is a professional mixologist in the early stages of his career. With just five years (at the time of writing) under his belt, he is already demonstrating the skills that set him apart as one of the world's best. In 2011, whilst still undergoing his academic studies, he competed in the Vibe Mixology and Flair competition and placed third, coming in ahead of many skilled bartenders with years of experience behind them. In his first few years he worked at the Sofitel Luxury Resort and Hotel in Bali, graduating rapidly from bartender to specialist mixologist. His Diageo World Class win is his current career highlight and resulted in him receiving the title of Indonesian Bartender of the Year.

NOLET'S BEACH
RYU FUJII

Ryu says: *My cocktail was inspired by the Tiki style of cocktail.*
World Class 2016 opened in Miami and so I decided that a Tiki drink under the sun
would be perfect. I made special glassware, similar to the Tiki style.
The taste was based on Ketel One's flavour. The freshness is from the juices,
the silkiness from orgeat, and umami is from the vinegar.

50ML KETEL ONE VODKA
15ML HOMEMADE ORGEAT*
20ML HONEY-PINEAPPLE JUICE**
10ML FRESH LEMON JUICE
1 TSP WHITE WINE VINEGAR

METHOD: Add all the ingredients to a shaker with scoop of ice and shake well. Strain into a martini glass and garnish with a spray of absinthe and a star anise.

HOMEMADE ORGEAT*
Combine 100ml unsweetened almond milk with 100g sugar in a pan and gently warm. Add 1 tsp of vanilla extract and 10ml orange flower water and stir until the sugar is dissolved. Cool and store in an airtight bottle.

HONEY-PINEAPPLE JUICE**
Combine 200ml pineapple juice with 50ml honey in a pan and simmer for 5 minutes. Allow to cool completely, then keep chilled (tends to keep for 1 day maximum).

————

RYU FUJII's mixology career began in 2003 as a bartender at the Rude Bar in Kobe. By 2006 he was working at Bar K in Osaka, one of Japan's most famous classic cocktail and bourbon bars, and where, more than a decade later, he is the manager and head bartender. After completing his Elite Bartenders qualification in 2011 he began his competitive mixology career, focusing on the Diageo World Class event. Ryu made the national finals three years in a row between 2011 and 2013 and also managed to become the Speed Challenge winner in 2012. His breakthrough year was 2016 when, at his fourth attempt, he became the national champion and went on to represent Japan in the global finals, placing as runner-up and officially being recognised as the number-two mixologist in the world for 2016.

WINNER OF DIAGEO WORLD CLASS JAPAN 2016 (2ND PLACE AT GLOBAL FINALS)

NOVA AMARA
PRAMOD MOHITE

Pramod says: *My inspiration was the classic Negroni and the flavour characteristics of Campari. I tried to combine the flavours in a well-balanced drink and use the influence of my customers' feedback when I presented the cocktail to them. With additional feedback from my bar manager at Buddha Bar, I eventually refined my recipe and created the drink that would go on to win the competition. Nova Amara means 'New Lovely'.*

5 BASIL LEAVES
30ML CAMPARI
20ML PISCO
15ML GRAND MARNIER
10ML MERLOT RED WINE

METHOD: 'Slap' the basil leaves and add them to a mixing glass. Add a scoop of ice and the remaining ingredients and stir for 10 seconds. Strain into a coupette glass and garnish with grapefruit peel.

———————

PRAMOD MOHITE graduated from the Hospitality Institute of Mumbai and began his bartending career in 2010. He started by working in bars as a bar-back and then enrolled on a dedicated cocktail course where he learned the essentials of cocktail mixology. In 2012 he received his big break when offered the role of bartender at the Chelsea Plaza Hotel in Dubai. While at the Chelsea Plaza, Pramod started competing in a range of different cocktail mixology and flair-tending competitions. However, his major passion has always been for the classic Negroni cocktail, and when the opportunity to compete in Campari's Negroni competition presented itself he grasped it with both hands. The rest is history!

WINNER OF CAMPARI NEGRONI COMPETITION 2015

PAN-MALAYAN TEA
SHAWN CHONG

Shawn says: *For this cocktail, I wanted to bring local elements to the drink that would represent my heritage: I am Malaysian–Chinese. Also, I have travelled extensively and wanted to incorporate an ingredient that is used globally. The pandan represents Malaysia or Malaya and the guok poh tea represents the Chinese part. The cinnamon is used in international cuisine and so represents the bridge to the world. And lastly, the whisky has been a big part of the drinking culture in Malaysia for generations.*

40ML JOHNNIE WALKER GOLD LABEL WHISKY
20ML PANDAN CINNAMON SYRUP*
30ML CHRYSANTHEMUM PU ERH TEA (GUOK POH)**

METHOD: Add all the ingredients to a shaker tin and throw*** the cocktail approximately 10 times. Pour into a Chinese tea cup and garnish with amaranth tea flower (or any other dried tea flower).

PANDAN CINNAMON SYRUP*
Combine 100g palm sugar, 100ml water, 1 cinnamon stick and 1 pandan leaf together in a pan and bring to the boil for 1 minute. Remove from the heat and allow to cool.

CHRYSANTHEMUM PU ERH TEA**
Add 2 chrysanthemum pu erh tea bags to 200ml hot water. Steep for 10 minutes, then remove the tea bags and allow to cool. (If unable to get pre-packed tea, use 1 tsp of loose pu erh tea leaves and about 8 dried chrysanthemum flowers.)

THROW***
For this method, you will require two shaker tins (or you can use the tin and glass from a single shaker). First, chill the tins in a freezer for a minimum of 10 minutes prior to mixing the drink. Add the ingredients to one of the tins and then pour back and forth between the tins for the required number of times.

————

SHAWN CHONG began his hospitality career in 2008 as a team member at the Hilton Hotel in Kuala Lumpur. By 2010 he was the manager at Hoofed Restaurant and a year later had moved into food and beverage lecturing at the Sunway University, a position that he held for three years. In 2013, Shawn became co-owner and bartender at Omakase + Appreciate and by 2016 had taken the role of academy director at the RAD Academy, Malaysia. Shawn is arguably one of the most dominant competitors on the Asian cocktail scene. He has won the Diageo World Class Malaysia title on no fewer than three occasions (2009, 2011 and 2015), was the winner of the Gold Excellence Award at Cullinaire Malaysia 2009, and of course became the grand champion at the 2015 Diageo World Class for the entire South-East Asia region.

WINNER OF DIAGEO WORLD CLASS SOUTH-EAST ASIA 2015

PINEAPPLE & RUM THYME SOUR
ADAM SCHELL

Adam says: *This cocktail was created because I enjoy using herbs and spices in fresh, vibrant cocktails. I think thyme lends itself to being used with sweeter flavours, and pineapple is fragrant and sweet, not requiring any additional sugar. The sweetness of the pineapple will determine how much lime is required. Balance of taste is needed. Customers appreciate that level of detail.*

6 x 1cm chunks fresh pineapple
20ml fresh lime juice
45ml Havana Añejo Especial Rum
20ml Giffard Thym Liqueur
¼ egg white

METHOD: In a shaker, muddle the pineapple and lime. Add the remaining ingredients with a scoop of ice and shake. Strain into a short glass Garnish with a small sprig of thyme.

NOTE FROM PAUL: *The cocktail was presented in the competition in a highball as it was a long drink comp, but it's better served short.*

———————

ADAM SCHELL has worked in cocktail bars for nearly 20 years. He has twice won the Queensland Long Drink Competition in Australia, placing third nationally. He describes his technique as 'trying to use an ingredient against what it is usually used for', and believes this is what sets him apart as an innovative mixologist. Examples of this creative streak are using a smoked salt rim on a grilled orange, and developing a chilli margarita to represent the taste of Australia. Adam is a true believer in service being more important than mixing drinks and spends much of his time working with young bartenders to help develop customer interaction abilities. As he says, 'You're not always going to be needed to make cocktails, but customer service, knowledge and speed are always needed'.

WINNER OF AUSTRALIAN BARTENDERS GUILD LONG DRINK COMPETITION 2016

THE PINEAPPLE MARTINI
BEN REED

Ben says: *The Pineapple Martini was created as a reaction to the infusion craze of the 90s. Bartenders were sticking everything under the sun into bottles of vodka, from garlic and chillies to Skittles and Mars bars – I think someone even tried smoked salmon. We were the first to experiment with fresh fruit with the Pineapple Martini and went on to create a whole menu of them at the Met bar – a new craze was born.*

4 RIPE PINEAPPLE CHUNKS
60ML ABSOLUT VODKA
5ML SUGAR SYRUP

METHOD: Muddle the pineapple chunks in a shaker. Add a scoop of ice and the remaining ingredients. Shake hard and double strain in to a martini glass. Garnish with a pineapple leaf.

NOTE FROM PAUL: *Whilst this drink is 20 years old now, I have included it as it defined the direction in which the UK cocktail scene travelled as we moved into the 21st century. Its simplistic genius changed the way we thought about cocktails thereafter.*

———————

Ben Reed is a leading light in the generation that defined UK bar culture. For over 25 years, Ben has been at the forefront of the global drinks industry and is recognised internationally as a spirit expert and passionate spokesperson for cocktails. From running the ground-breaking Met Bar in the mid-90s to setting up London's first cocktail consultancy in 2000, his 14 books have sold over a million copies in 25 countries and he makes regular TV appearances, including presenting a 13-episode series on cocktails for the BBC. His weekly 'Barfly' column featured in *The Times Magazine* for two years and he has written for the *Guardian*, *Vogue* and *GQ*. At Cocktail Credentials, Ben acts as a consultant to the world's biggest drinks brands, writing, training and speaking about cocktails all over the world. As an educator, he has trained more than 15,000 bartenders in 20 countries and his professional bartender training programmes and bespoke courses are acknowledged globally as being leaders in their field and have set the benchmark for the industry standard across all sectors of the bar world.

WINNER OF ABSOLUT COCKTAIL COMPETITION 1997

PLAYA FORTUNA
RYAN WAINWRIGHT

Ryan says: *The inspiration for Playa Fortuna is just that: the place.*
My girlfriend surprised me with two tickets to Puerto Rico. It was right before the
competition submission deadline and I found myself just off the coast of Playa Fortuna
sipping a coconut. It was with that in mind that I wanted to create something that
was honestly Puerto Rican, while at the same time never losing sight of the rum,
the true star of the show. This drink is all about an honest representation.

40ML BACARDI SUPERIOR RUM
20ML FRESH LIME JUICE
20ML COCONUT WATER CORDIAL*
7ML FALERNUM
4 DROPS HYDRATED TARTARIC ACID**

METHOD: Add all the ingredients to a shaker with a scoop of ice and shake well. Strain into a Nick & Nora glass and garnish with a marigold.

COCONUT WATER CORDIAL*
Stir 50g sugar into 50ml coconut water until dissolved.

HYDRATED TARTARIC ACID**
Mix 20ml water with 5ml cream of tartar until smooth.

———————

RYAN WAINWRIGHT is a cocktail purist with a clean, minimalist style. Born in Southern California, Ryan attended university in Sacramento to study photography. After stumbling upon an opportunity to bartend at a concert in Big Sur, he found his true calling. He moved to Los Angeles in 2010, where he worked at notable restaurants like Gjelina and The Tasting Kitchen before joining the Bombet Hospitality Group in 2014. His attention to detail has garnered him much acclaim in both the Los Angeles and national drink landscapes, including numerous Best Bartender and Best Bar Programme awards. On the mixology front, Ryan has wins for the Southern California region at the United States Bartenders' Guild's Most Imaginative Bartender Competition alongside national awards at the various competitions including The Maestro Lucano Cocktail Competition. Ryan is now one of Los Angeles' most sought after bartenders and is currently the director of bar programmes for Bombet Hospitality.

78

QUEEN ANNE'S LACE
ANDREW MELTZER

Andrew says: *Queen Anne's Lace is undoubtedly a brunch-time cocktail. It's meant to be a lighter alternative to the Bloody Mary. This cocktail is inspired by the fresh produce abundant in Northern California. Our carrots taste bright and fresh, and I pass by wild fennel every day on my walk to work. I've added the springtime flavour of blooming flowers, and brightened things up with a dash of fresh lemon juice and absinthe.*

45ML KETEL ONE VODKA
25ML FRESH CARROT JUICE
10ML FRESH LEMON JUICE
10ML THYME SYRUP*
5ML IRIS LIQUEUR**
1 DASH ABSINTHE

METHOD: Combine all ingredients in a cocktail shaker with a scoop of ice. Shake quickly and fine-strain into a chilled Irish coffee glass. Garnish with a sprig of thyme, a fennel frond, or a small edible flower.

THYME SYRUP*
Combine 500g sugar with 350ml filtered water in a small saucepan set over low heat. Add 6 sprigs of fresh thyme and stir regularly until the sugar has dissolved. Remove from the heat and let cool for 1 hour, then strain and discard the thyme. Store in an airtight container in the refrigerator for up to 2 weeks. A fennel bulb (chopped) is a great alternative to thyme.

If iris liqueur** is unavailable, substitute an elderflower liqueur such as St. Germain.

————

ANDREW MELTZER, aka 'Daiquiri Doctor', fell in love with organic food and craft beverages at an Atlanta brewpub. However, it was a fateful move to San Francisco in 2012 that launched his cocktail career at 15 Romolo. He is an active community member and leader of the United States Bartenders' Guild, San Francisco, having been president since 2016 and VP since 2014. He was a national finalist of Bacardi Legacy in 2014 and 2015, global finalist of Domaine de Canton in 2014 and winner of the Diageo World Class, USA in 2015 and 2016. Andrew is inspired by the abundant local San Francisco produce, artists and California hipsters. With a reputation for producing great Daiquiris, Andrew knew that his mission was complete when a guest recently said, 'I really like this drink, I'm going to start ordering Daiquiris wherever I go.'

WINNER OF DIAGEO WORLD CLASS USA 2016

QUEEN B
REGERI ZOO

Regeri says: *The inspiration for my drink came from having to mix a drink for the Queen B herself, Beyoncé. Back then I was really hyped about an ingredient called oleo saccharum (sugar and lemon zest). In her album* Lemonade, *Beyoncé gives her own recipe for the perfect lemonade. One of the ingredients is basically oleo saccharum! Creole Bitters gives the taste of her Louisiana Creole heritage and the bee pollen represents what she has become – the Queen B.*

50ML DON JULIO BLANCO TEQUILA
15ML BEE-POLLEN SYRUP*
10ML OLEO SACCHARUM**
30ML FRESH LEMON JUICE
4 DASHES THE BITTER TRUTH CREOLE BITTERS

METHOD: Add all the ingredients to a shaker with a scoop of ice and shake hard. Double strain into a coupe glass and garnish with your favourite flower blossom.

BEE-POLLEN SYRUP*
Heat 8g bee pollen in a pan until you start to smell the aroma. Add 200ml water and 200g sugar and bring to the boil, whisking thoroughly. Strain through a muslin cloth and allow to cool. Keep refrigerated.

OLEO SACCHARUM**
Add the peel of 8 lemons (remove any pith) to 200g caster sugar. Seal in a airtight bag and allow to rest for 24 hours. Remove the lemon peel and store in an airtight container.

————————

REGERI ZOO's first encounter with bartending came while living in the UK and working in a local Birmingham-based bar collecting glasses. There he saw, and eventually mixed, his first Mojito. Upon his return to Estonia in 2011, he started working at a new bar called Meat Market where they enrolled him on a month-long cocktail course. Regeri started to enter as many cocktail competitions as possible in a quest to develop his skills and expose himself to the talents of Estonia's best bartenders of the time. His first success came in a non-alcoholic cocktail competition run by Giffard syrups. Shortly after that, in 2015, Regeri entered and won the Estonian Bacardi Legacy Competition, which gave him the opportunity to compete in the global finals in Sydney, Australia. This success gave him a major confidence boost and one year later he had become the Diageo World Class champion for Estonia. His goal is to raise bartending to a level that Estonia has never seen before.

WINNER OF DIAGEO WORLD CLASS ESTONIA 2016

RAIN OR SHINE
ORMAN BAG-AO

Orman says: *This cocktail is inspired by the Mojito cocktail, which happened to be the first cocktail that I learned during my early days as a bartender. The taste inspired me to pursue my passion in bartending. This version adds a twist of guava juice that balances the acidity from the lime. Its carrot juice properties provide a refreshing, flavoursome, mouth-watering effect while you sip. A dash of grapefruit bitters adds a delicate aroma and citrus notes, reminiscent of a summer experience.*

60ML BACARDI CARTA BLANCA RUM
30ML FRESH CARROT JUICE
15ML GUAVA JUICE
15ML FRESH LIME JUICE
15ML MINT SYRUP*
1 DASH GRAPEFRUIT BITTERS

METHOD: Add all the ingredients to a cocktail shaker with a scoop of ice. Shake well and strain into a coupette glass. Garnish with dehydrated carrot and a fresh mint sprig (optional).

MINT SYRUP*
Add 80g sugar to 50ml water and heat. Now add 5-6 fresh mint sprigs and stir until the sugar has dissolved and the mint has infused. Strain the liquid and leave to cool.

————

ORMAN BAG-AO has worked on the Longbar at the Raffles Hotel in Makati City since 2013. In that time, he has established himself as a skilled and talented mixologist and bartender. In 2014 he won the PAGCOR Philippines Flairtending competition and followed that up by representing Team Philippines in the South East Asia finals of Diageo World Class. In 2016 he became a finalist in the La Maison Cointreau national cocktail competition and one year later became the national champion at the Bacardi Legacy competition, going on to compete in the global finals in Berlin.

RHUBARB MARGARITA
ANDRI DAVÍÐ PÉTURSSON

Andri says: *I grew up eating fresh rhubarb during the spring time in Iceland. We ate it covered with sugar and we usually stole it from somebody's garden! It is even a saying in Iceland that rhubarb tastes much better if it's stolen. The drink is very simple. It relies totally on the acidity found in the rhubarb, so it is a perfect drink to make for anybody who has rhubarb in their garden or even better, has a neighbour who has some.*

40ML DON JULIO BLANCO TEQUILA
10ML RHUBARB LIQUEUR
10ML AGAVE SYRUP
20ML FRESH RHUBARB JUICE

METHOD: Add all the ingredients to a shaker with a scoop of ice. Shake well and fine strain into a chilled coupe glass. Garnish with salt-covered rhubarb.

———————

ANDRI DAVÍÐ PÉTURSSON is an Icelandic bartender of great skill. He won the national finals of Diageo World Class in Iceland in 2016 and competed in the Global Finals in Miami the same year. Born in 1988, Andri began working in the restaurant and bar industry at the age of 16 and has gone on to become one of the pioneers of the craft cocktail movement in Iceland. Today Andri works as a freelance bartender and runs a consulting company called The Viceman, specialising in helping to raise skills and standards across the Icelandic bar industry. He is also the vice president of the Icelandic Bartenders Guild (B.C.I.).

WINNER OF DIAGEO WORLD CLASS ICELAND 2016

SHUFFLE IN DUMAINE
BLAIR FRODELIUS

Blair says: *This is my tribute to the classic cocktails of New Orleans. These drinks tend to be powerful eye-openers that have a lot of character. Having spent a lot of time in the French Quarter, I also gained a love of NOLA jazz. The name 'Shuffle in Dumaine' comes from a song lyric by Jools Holland, which was his tribute to the sounds of New Orleans.*

I TSP FERNET-BRANCA
50ML RITTENHOUSE BOTTLED IN BOND RYE
I TSP DEMERARA SIMPLE SYRUP
2 DASHES THE BITTER TRUTH CREOLE BITTERS

METHOD: Fill a coupe glass with ice (no water) until chilled. Then empty the ice and rinse the coupe with Fernet-Branca, discarding any extra. Stir the rye, simple syrup and bitters with ice in a mixing glass and strain into the chilled and rinsed coupe. Then smile.

———————

BLAIR FRODELIUS is a walking encyclopaedia of drinks knowledge. He is a regular contributor to USBGPulse.com, Drinkwire.com and PAMAProfessional.com. He had the honour of having some of his original recipes published in the 75th anniversary edition of *Mr Boston Official Bartender's Guide*. He's a graduate of Pernod-Ricard's BarSmarts Live and BarSmarts Wired programmes and is a United States Bartenders' Guild Master Accredited Spirits Professional. His creative mixology has led to him presenting monthly cocktail masterclasses at Kitty Hoynes in New York. Blair is also a member of the Museum of the American Cocktail and author of the internationally recognised website, goodspritisnews.com. In addition to his award-winning cocktail, he has placed on the podium in a number of other competitions including the Woodford Reserve 'I'll Take Manhattan' competition 2010 and the Hukilau Rum Barrel Master Mixologist Competition 2011.

SIBELIUS DREAM
TORE BERGER

Tore says: *As a bartender with many years competing, I love to use the seasons in Scandinavia as my inspiration. Finlandia International is a big competition, and it was an honour to win the 'Long Drink' category. Fresh – Clean – Visual are three keywords for me when designing a new cocktail. In Norway we say, 'Skål', in Finland they say, 'Kippis' – Cheers!*

50ML FINLANDIA CRANBERRY VODKA
3 FRESH NORWEGIAN STRAWBERRIES
15ML KOSKENKORVA PEACH
50ML FRESH LEMON JUICE
1 DASH FRESH ORANGE JUICE
SPRITE, TO TOP UP

METHOD: Add the first four ingredients to a blender with a scoop of crushed ice. Blend until smooth and pour into a highball glass. Top up with a dash of fresh orange and Sprite. Garnish with orange peel, a strawberry and some lemon balm leaves.

———————

TORE BERGER spent the vast majority of his career working for Color Cruises. Starting in 1997, with ten year's hospitality and bar experience already behind him, he held the position of maître d' and bar manager on five different cruise ships, until 2014 when he made the decision to move 'ashore' once again. Since then, Tore has worked as consultant to the Vinmonopolet (the government-monopoly shops for spirits and wine). Tore has had a great deal of success in cocktail competitions over a sustained period of time. From a second place at the 1994 Finlandia Cup, numerous wins followed until he completed the circle in 2000 by becoming the Finlandia Cup champion. After a selection of additional top three places in competitions throughout 2002 and 2003, Tore 'retired' from the competition scene until 2012 when, in his forties, he reached the finals of the Koskenkorva Vodka and the Arvesølvet Aquavit competitions.

WINNER OF FINLANDIA CUP COCKTAIL COMPETITION, NORWAY 2000

84

SIN LIMITES
PETER GÓZON

Peter says: Sin Limites means limitless. It is also the emotion that people feel when we reach our dreams. When, for the first time, I saw bartenders working in one of the most epic bars here in Budapest, I was amazed; I wanted to be like them. I was scared and I thought I didn't have the skills to become so legendary. But I never gave up, and I fought until I reached my dream.

3 FRESH CARDAMOM PODS
45ML BACARDI CARTA BLANCA RUM
15ML HOMEMADE VANILLA SYRUP*
20ML FRESH LIME JUICE
5ML CAMPARI

METHOD: Add the cardamom pods to a shaker and crush using a pestle. Now add the remaining ingredients and a scoop of ice and shake well. Strain into a coupe glass with a Vanilla Salt** rim.

HOMEMADE VANILLA SYRUP*
Heat 250ml water with 250g sugar and 2 vanilla pods. Stir until the sugar has dissolved and the vanilla pods have infused. Allow to cool, then strain the liquid into a bottle.

VANILLA SALT**
Place 200g salt into a sealable plastic container along with 3 vanilla pods. Leave for a minimum of 3 days. NOTE: The longer you leave the salt the stronger the vanilla becomes.

PETER GÓZON began his career in 2014 as a waiter at the Berekai Art Studio. Quickly realising that serving drinks was his favourite part of the job, he made the switch to a bartending career and moved into hotel bartending. Over the following years, he moved up the bartending ladder, eventually working in high-level cocktails bars at venues like the Ritz-Carlton in Budapest. In 2016, Peter decided to test his skills in the world of competition bartending and immediately made an impact by placing as runner-up in the Jagermeister Cocktail competition. Later that year he placed first in a regional Monin Cup event that qualified him for the national competition, which he also won, becoming national champion. Subsequently, he represented his country at the global finals where he finished fourth. In 2017 he cemented his position as one of Hungary's most talented new mixologists by winning the national Bacardi Legacy competition.

WINNER OF BACARDI LEGACY HUNGARY 2017

SLOE MOTION
RON DE PRETER

Ron says: My inspiration was to create a modern drink based on a forgotten cocktail spirit (sloe gin) that deserved a comeback, combined with the trend of that time, which was fresh crushed fruit (Caipirinha style drinks).

½ FRESH LIME
¼ FRESH ORANGE
30ML WENNEKER SLOE GIN
30ML WENNEKER CURAÇAO ORANGE
80ML APPLE JUICE

METHOD: Cut the lime and orange into small pieces and muddle in a cocktail shaker. Add a scoop of crushed ice and the remaining ingredients. Shake well and pour into a tumbler. Garnish with orange, starfruit (or lime) and a cherry.

————————

RON DE PRETER is a Dutch bartender who was showed signs of his future career as a young boy by collecting liqueur bottles and displaying them on a self-made bar in his bedroom. By the age of 15 he had begun his career for real, working at a nightclub in his hometown. It was there he made his first cocktails. By 1993 he had joined the German Bartenders Association to gain access to their cocktail competitions and in his first year won the German Long Drink Competition. Ron was then recruited as global brand ambassador by Wenneker distilleries, a position that he still holds today. Many competition wins followed, including victory in the Cocktail Speed Cup and gaining the Prestige Award (for best cocktail mixing technique) for 2001 in Germany. By 2002 Ron had also joined the Netherlands Bartenders Association and in his first Dutch competition won the Prestige Award there too. He is the winner of numerous other titles including two Dutch National Cocktail Championships.

WINNER OF INTERNATIONAL COCKTAIL CHALLENGE 2003

SLOW GRIND
JAMES BARKER

∽

James says: *Slow Grind is a drink which gives you the chance to enjoy Tanqueray, at any time of day. It brings together the increasingly exciting worlds of craft cocktails and craft coffee in the form of a portable, spirituous caffeine fix to give the drinker the edge they need in the hustle that is modern-day life.*

90ML INDIAN TONIC WATER, CHILLED
30ML TANQUERAY NO. TEN GIN
30ML ETHIOPIAN SIAMO HUNKUTE COLD BREW COFFEE*
10ML SALTED EARL GREY TEA SYRUP**

METHOD: Pour the chilled tonic water into a small aluminium bottle (or you can use a glass). Add the gin, Cold Brew Coffee and the Earl Grey Syrup to a shaker with a scoop of ice and roll (not shake) three times. Strain into the bottle. Garnish with grapefruit zest.

NOTE FROM PAUL: *For the competition, James sealed the bottle and placed in a paper bag with a club sandwich and a pack of ready salted crisps. He then sealed the bag with a 'meal deal' sticker and served.*

COLD BREW COFFEE*
Infuse 260ml hot (90ºC) water with 20g ground Ethiopian Siamo Hunkute coffee beans for 3 minutes, then strain and refrigerate for 24 hours.

SALTED EARL GREY SYRUP**
Infuse 7g loose leaf Earl Grey tea in 250ml hot (90ºC) water for 5 minutes, then strain and stir in 200g white sugar and 1g salt until it dissolves. Refrigerate.

———————

JAMES BARKER began his bartending career in London in 2011, making the move to Kuala Lumpur two years later, where he worked as head bartender for the Santai Resort, achieving the accolade of Kuala Lumpur's Best Bar. Another career move followed as he stepped out from behind the bar in late 2015 to work for a Hong Kong based hospitality consultancy, providing bar training and cocktail-menu development for a range of high-profile hotels. James is held in very high regard in the region and, as such, has organised and judged numerous cocktail competitions, including the La Maison Cointreau Cocktail Competition. James's win in the 2016 Hong Kong & Macau, Diageo World Class event saw him travel to Miami for the global finals where he won the Shape of Cocktail to Come category. James is currently the group bar specialist for the JIA group in Hong Kong, responsible for the bar training and direction across multiple venues.

WINNER OF DIAGEO WORLD CLASS HONG KONG & MACAU 2016

SMOKED AGED OF APERITIVO

FELIX PATRISIUS SANI

Felix says: *My inspiration for this cocktail comes from the fact that I love to drink the iconic Negroni with an Indonesian cigarette. Indonesian cigarettes are always mixed with cloves. I decided to mimic the Negroni style but combine a Ron de Zacapa rum with Vermouth, Aperol and my homemade Winter Syrup with orange bitters. And of course, the most important thing was to represent Indonesia as a 'Heaven of Spice'.*

CINNAMON, CLOVES AND STAR ANISE, FOR SMOKING
40ML RON ZACAPA 23 RUM
10ML VERMOUTH DRAPO ROSSO
10ML APEROL
10ML WINTER SYRUP*
5ML ORANGE BITTERS

METHOD: Firstly prepare an old-fashioned glass by chilling it with ice, then smoking with a smoke gun** charged with cinnamon, cloves and anise.

Add all the ingredients to a mixing glass filled with ice. Stir for 10 seconds and then add some smoke from the smoke gun into the mixing glass and cover with a napkin. Swirl the mixture a little, then strain in to the prepared glass. Garnish with a twist of orange.

WINTER SYRUP*
Crush 30g whole allspice berries in a mortar until they are coarsely ground. Place them in a sealable glass jar along with 250ml Ron Zacapa rum. Allow to steep for 4 days, shaking daily. On day 5, add 1 cinnamon stick (broken into pieces) to the mixture and continue to steep for a further 7 days. On day 12, strain through a coffee filter and retain the liquid in a bottle. Heat 400ml water with 100g brown sugar until the sugar has dissolved completely. Allow the syrup to cool,

then add it to the rum infusion mixture. Shake and leave to rest for another 2 days.

Smoke guns** are available online from suppliers of kitchen equipment or from dedicated barware suppliers.

————

FELIX PATRISIUS SANI is a well-travelled bartender, having worked since 2010 in locations such as Surabaya, Qatar, Bahrain, Dubai and Bali, where he is currently the manager of operations for Mint. He has been a finalist at the Bacardi Legacy competition, won second place in the Monin Mixology Championships and was the overall champion at the De Kuyper Masters. Felix has a reputation for creating sophisticated and complex blends and often includes ingredients that can take many days to prepare in advance. This award-winner is a perfect example of this attention to detail.

SHOOTING STAR
PAUL MARTIN

Paul says: As the author of this book it seemed appropriate to include one of my own award-winning drinks. This one represents an era when the current focus on highly sophisticated techniques and mixes was in its infancy. As such, the simplicity of this drink perfectly reflects the more relaxed mood of the later part of the 20th century. It tastes wonderful and looks great and is still one of my favourite career memories.

30ML BEEFEATER GIN
15ML ARCHER'S PEACH SCHNAPPS
30ML CRANBERRY JUICE
20ML ORANGE JUICE
10ML GRENADINE SYRUP
30ML DOUBLE (HEAVY) CREAM
20ML CRÈME DE BANANE LIQUEUR

METHOD: Add the gin, schnapps, cranberry juice, orange juice and grenadine to a shaker with a scoop of ice. Shake well and strain into a trumpet glass, leaving the top quarter of the glass free for the second layer. Now stir the cream and banana liqueur together (no ice) and gently float the mixture on top of the drink. Garnish by sprinkling ground cinnamon through a template* to create a star on the drink's surface.

To create the template*, simply cut a star shape from a piece of card.

———————

MY WONDERFUL JOURNEY began over 30 years ago in a small wine bar. Over the following years, I worked in most of London's top cocktail bars, eventually opening my own bar Kudos in South West London in 1991. Kudos ran successfully for three years, then I sold up and established a new career as one of the UK's first cocktail and mixology consultants – a role unheard of at the time! This work led to me developing and running bartender training courses, which for the last 20 years has resulted in me coaching over 30,000 of the world's bartenders and hospitality professionals. I have written six cocktail and bartending-skills books including *The World Encyclopaedia of Cocktails* and, of course, this book! I've presented more than a dozen instructional DVDs, have made more than 50 TV appearances, held two Guinness World Records for cocktail speed-mixing and have won 7 global mixology competitions including with this drink, the first victory of my career. At the time of writing, I have the best-selling online cocktail course on Udemy.com.

WINNER OF VINEXPO INTERNATIONAL COCKTAIL CHALLENGE 1997

SURPRISE ME
LOREEN HERNANDEZ

Loreen says: *The inspiration for my cocktail was from a 'gin and tonic cart' where I worked. With this, the guest may choose any gin, tonic, fruits, herbs and spices of their preference, which is then served in the style of Spanish G&T. I got the cocktail's name from some guests who would say 'surprise me' instead of making their own selections. This drink is my response to that request.*

1 CUBE FRESH YOUNG GINGER
50ML TANQUERAY LONDON DRY GIN
10ML FRESH LEMON JUICE
10ML MONIN LEMON TEA SYRUP
TONIC WATER, TO TOP UP

METHOD: Muddle the ginger with the gin in a mixing glass. Next add the lemon juice, lemon tea syrup and a scoop of ice. Stir and double strain into an ice-filled goblet. Top with tonic and serve with a lime twist and cinnamon sticks.

———

LOREEN HERNANDEZ has worked in the hospitality industry since 2010, when as an intern she won the Best Waitress award. However, regardless of her apparent waiting skills, is wasn't long before the allure of the bar drew her in a different direction, and since 2011 she has tended bar at Rambla, Crystal Lounge and Pacha in the Philippines. Her 2014 Monin Mixology Cup victory saw her represent the Philippines in the Asia Pacific finals where she performed well. In 2015 Loreen won the Cocktail Art category at the Macau Bartender of the Year competition and followed that up by reaching the finals of the Diageo World Class, Hong Kong & Macau event in 2016.

WINNER OF MONIN MIXOLOGY CUP PHILIPPINES 2014

177

TENDER 10
STEVE LEONG

Steve says: *Tess Bar & Kitchen is situated along Seah Street, home to one of the most famous chicken rice restaurants in Singapore. As a tribute to the heritage of the area, I have created a Hainanese Chicken Rice-inspired cocktail that embraces all the key ingredients of the popular dish.*

60ML TANQUERAY NO. TEN GIN
30ML LA QUINTINYE EXTRA DRY VERMOUTH
22ML CHICKEN RICE LIQUEUR*

METHOD: Add all the ingredients to a mixing glass with a scoop of ice and stir. Strain into a bowl over a large ice cube and garnish with a sprig of parsley and some lemon zest. Serve with a chicken drumstick.

CHICKEN RICE LIQUEUR*
Combine 300ml King's Ginger Liqueur, 50g fresh ginger, 100ml sesame oil, 15 cloves garlic and 20 stalks of Chinese parsley in a vacuum-sealed bag. Cook sous vide at 45°C for 2 hours. Strain and allow to cool at room temperature.

STEVE LEONG (aka Uncle Leong) started his bartending career at Loof in Singapore in 2009 and since then has worked in a number of pioneering bars. In 2013 he was a semi-finalist in both the La Maison Cointreau and Giffard Singapore cocktail competitions before reaching the finals of the Vedrenne Cocktail Grand Prix in the same year. By 2014 he had won his first competition at the Tanqueray Ten Challenge. His most successful year to date by far was 2015. First, he won the Haig Club Whisky Challenge, which resulted in him headlining the Singapore launch of Haig Club alongside David Beckham. He then became champion at the Belvedere Martini Challenge and finally won the Diageo World Class Singapore event. The latter of which led to him also being crowned the champion for the South East Asia region. Steve is now a World Class ambassador and was a member of the judging panel for the 2016 event.

WINNER OF DIAGEO WORLD CLASS SINGAPORE 2015

THAI THAI

PAILIN (MILK) SAJJANIT

Pailin says: *My inspiration for this cocktail challenge was to create a cocktail made from local ingredients that best represented my country.*

20ML KHAO MAK (SWEET FERMENTED JASMINE RICE)
50ML KETEL ONE VODKA
10ML KAFFIR LIME SYRUP
15ML FRESH LIME JUICE
2 DASHES GRAPEFRUIT BITTERS

METHOD: Combine all the ingredients with 50g crushed ice in a blender. Blend at high speed until smooth, then pour into a silver mug. Garnish with a lime wheel.

———————

PAILIN SAJJANIT's background is in the hotels of Bangkok where he was part of the pre-opening team for the Sofitel. In a short but dynamic career, he moved on to the Vesper Bar and then to the Il Fumo, part of the Vesper group. He is now the group bar manager overseeing both venue's bar operations. In 2011 Pailin won his first competition, The Ultimate Ketel One Cosmopolitan Martini competition. He has since gone on to win the Diplomatico Global 2015, Diageo World Class Thailand 2016 (in addition to the South East Asia title in the same year), was named Thailand's Best Bartender for 2016 and was winner of the 2016 Best Local Flavours Challenge. Pailin also works as a bartender trainer, running masterclasses and courses for Thailand's bartender community.

THE ALCHEMIST
LAURA DUCA

Laura says: *The inspiration for my drink was the art of bartending and how close that comes to alchemy. Taking a spirit and breaking it down to its core flavours and then using them to create something totally different, each ingredient that goes into the drink represents the flavours found in the rum.*

40ml Ron Zacapa Rum
10ml Amaro Averna
5ml Amontillado sherry
5ml Pedro Ximénez
5ml crème de cacao white
Smoked whisky spray (an Islay whisky)

METHOD: Add all the ingredients to a mixing glass except the whisky and stir. Chill one rocks glass and perfume it with the whisky. Strain the drink into the glass over a single large ice chunk. Serve along with a Gorgonzola cheese 'candy' filled with Pedro Ximénez soaked raisins and coated with caramelised hazelnuts*.

*Soak the raisins in Pedro Ximénez for 24 hours, then chop. Shape some Gorgonzola into a ball, make a hollow inside and fill with the chopped raisins. Coat in crushed caramelised hazelnuts.

———————

LAURA DUCA is originally from Romania but has been living and working as a bartender in Dubai since 2011. She began as a waitress in a small bar called Vintage, but quickly moved behind the bar and 'fell in love' with the bartending profession. In 2012 Laura moved to the Embassy Club at the Grosvenor House Hotel, one of Dubai's busiest nightspots. It was here that her career began to rocket and she entered her first cocktail competition with a drink that is still featured on the menu today. In 2014 Laura made her first attempt at entering the Diageo World Class event and managed to get all the way to the final. Her competition performances continued until in 2015 she won the UAE La Maison Cointreau competition and went on to represent her country in the global finals in Bangkok, finishing third. In addition to this, in the same year she also placed third in the Dons of Tequila competition in Mexico. Her 2016 win in Diageo World Class is the pinnacle of her competition career so far.

WINNER OF DIAGEO WORLD CLASS UAE 2016

THE BELL OF JALISCO

MIKE MCGINTY

Mike says: I got the inspiration for my cocktail from understanding the time and effort that goes into the creation of every single drop of Patrón; I wanted to create a serve dedicated to the men and women that are involved in the creation of this ultra-premium tequila. The name of my cocktail is a reference to the bell peppers that have been used and the belief that Patrón is the 'belle' of Jalisco.

30ML PATRÓN REPOSADO TEQUILA
12.5ML CHAMOMILE-INFUSED DRY VERMOUTH*
25ML GRAPEFRUIT IPA
20ML FRESH LEMON JUICE
20ML YELLOW BELL PEPPER SHRUB**

METHOD: Add all ingredients to a cocktail shaker with a scoop of ice. Shake well and double strain into a glass. Garnish with a dehydrated lime and chamomile flowers.

CHAMOMILE-INFUSED DRY VERMOUTH*
Infuse 50g dried chamomile flowers in 700ml dry vermouth. Allow to steep for 2 hours and then strain.

YELLOW BELL PEPPER SHRUB**
Roast 500g yellow peppers in the oven at 150°C, until soft. Allow them to cool and then add them to 500g caster sugar, 5g smoked sea salt and 150ml sherry vinegar. Give it a good mix and leave for 3 days, mixing it every day. Finally, strain and chill.

———

MIKE MCGINTY started bartending at the Ninety-Nine Bar and Kitchen in Aberdeen in 2009. A three-year period at Treacle followed, where he eventually reached the position of general manager, before moving on to open The Voyage of Buck, a popular bar and restaurant in the West End of Edinburgh in 2016. Mike's career is littered with activities designed to promote the cocktail scene in his native Scotland. He is a joint founder of the Aberdeen Bartender's Club and a familiar face at many of Scotland's food and drink festivals, including running cocktail presentations and demonstrations at (among others) the Taste of Scotland festival. Mike's first competition success came in the 2010 Caorunn Gin Cocktail Competition (an achievement he repeated in 2016) and was followed by reaching the finals of Diageo World Class, Western Europe in 2012. In 2016 after becoming the UK Patrón Perfectionist champion, Mike entered the Global Patrón Perfectionist Competition where he defeated numerous other national winners to become the global champion of 2016.

WINNER OF PATRÓN PERFECTIONIST COCKTAIL COMPETITION, UK FINALS 2016

THE EASTERN MYTH
SOUFIANE EL ALAOUI

Soufiane says: *My drink was inspired by the flashy lifestyles of the young and wealthy people I meet in the Middle East, along with the Western culture of infusion and mixing. Combined together, they create this attractive eye-catching drink that is reminiscent of the great age of Middle Eastern spice and herb trading.*

45ML ROSEMARY AND SAFFRON INFUSED GIN*
25ML LIMONCELLO
15ML HOMEMADE ROSEMARY SYRUP**
5ML ROSEWATER
30ML EGG WHITE

METHOD: Add all the ingredients except the egg white to a shaker with a scoop of ice. Shake well, then strain the liquid into the shaker glass and discard the ice. Now add the egg white, close the shaker and shake well again (reverse dry shake). Fine strain into a coupe glass and garnish with a burnt rosemary sprig.

ROSEMARY AND SAFFRON INFUSED GIN*
Infuse 100ml gin with 2 sprigs of rosemary and 4 strands of saffron for 5 minutes, then strain. Store in a sealed bottle until required.

HOMEMADE ROSEMARY SYRUP**
Combine 500ml water with 500g sugar and 5 sprigs of rosemary in a pan and bring to the boil. Simmer gently for 5-6 minutes, then allow to cool. Strain into a sealable container and keep chilled.

———————

SOUFIANE EL ALAOUI began his career back in 2005 working as a bar-back at the Hilton Hotel in Morocco. Within a year, he had become a fully-fledged bartender working at the Theatro Club in Marrakesh. However, Soufiane felt that to truly develop his bartending skills he would also need to spread his wings and so, by 2009, he was working behind the bar of the Sheraton Deira Hotel in Dubai. Since then, Soufiane has remained in Dubai where he has held senior positions such as the role of manager and mixologist at the Cavalli Club. Dubai has also given Soufiane the opportunity to demonstrate his mixology skills as he has entered and won the Dubai Hendrick's Cup and both the Jameson's and Belvedere Cocktail Competitions. His Gin Mare Competition victory saw his first outside of Dubai.

THE KEY HOLDER
ELIAS STERGIOPOULOS

Elias says: *The first time I visited London, I was strolling around and I saw a sign on the door of a garden. It read, 'Private garden, key holders only'. This became the inspiration for my drink. Fresh ripe puréed pineapple along with lemon juice blended harmoniously with the dry and citrus character of Beefeater London Dry Gin. Kirsch and roses give a tangy, yet flowery depth as a finish to this drink.*

60ML BEEFEATER LONDON DRY GIN
10ML FRESH LEMON JUICE
10ML PINEAPPLE PURÉE (PREFERABLY HOMEMADE)
2 BSP SUGAR INFUSED WITH ROSE POWDER*
3ML GABRIEL BOUDIER KIRSCH
2 DASHES ANGOSTURA BITTERS

METHOD: Add all the ingredients to a mixing tin and stir gently until the sugar completely dissolves. Add a scoop of ice and shake rapidly. Fine strain into a chilled coupette glass (or tumbler) and garnish with dried rose petals.

SUGAR INFUSED WITH ROSE POWDER*
Combine 500g caster sugar with 2 tbsp rose powder in an airtight container. Allow to infuse for a minimum of 4 days, shaking the container once a day.

————

ELIAS STERGIOPOULOS has been bartending for more than ten years. Over the last four years he has been head bartender of Baba Au Rum in Athens and has been instrumental in helping them to appear in the annual World's 50 Best Bars list for both 2013 and 2016. In this role, Elias was also involved in organising the Athens Rum Festival. Elias has a fascination with the spirit pisco, and has written about it in *Fine Drinking* magazine. This passion has led to him moving to Peru to increase his knowledge and undertake training apprenticeships with numerous pisco-producing distilleries. In addition to winning MIXLDN in 2014, Elias was also the runner-up in the Havana Club Grand Prix. His drink was also featured in Gary Regan's *101 Best New Cocktails* in 2015.

THE RISK
CONSTANTINOS KAZELIS

Constantinos says: *The 'inspiration' was actually there all along.*
Skinos MCC is a team challenge, and as we all know it takes two to tango.
My colleague Alexis Argyrou and I have worked together for years, and to be honest
we are very loud and funny... Jokers if I may. So we created a presentation and
cocktail that reflects our own personalities and our teamwork.

30ML SKINOS MASTIHA SPIRIT
40ML DRY VERMOUTH FAT-WASHED WITH PARMESAN CHEESE*
25ML TOMATO WATER CORDIAL**
10ML GIN MARE
5 FRESH BASIL LEAVES

METHOD: Add all the ingredients to a two-piece shaker with a scoop of ice and shake very hard to break down all the basil leaves. Fine strain into an un-chilled Cognac snifter with a chunk of ice and garnish with an oyster leaf.

DRY VERMOUTH PARMESAN*
Sous vide 1 litre dry vermouth with 100g Parmesan cheese at 85°C for 30 minutes, then refrigerate until the Parmesan turns solid and strain through a muslin.

TOMATO WATER CORDIAL**
Blanch 300g tomatos to remove the skins, then cut them in half and remove the seeds. Add the tomatoes to a blender and purée until completely smooth, then add to a pan and bring to the boil; simmer for 3 minutes. Remove from heat and pass through a muslin cloth. The liquid will be clear 'tomato water'. Now mix the tomato water with 200g sugar, a dash (1ml) of citric acid, two dashes (2ml) of malic acid and a pinch of salt. Stir until the sugar has dissolved and then chill.

CONSTANTINOS KAZELIS is one of our less experienced mixologists and yet demonstrates great creative mixing with this award winner. He began in 2012 working as a bar-back, both mornings and evenings, for the bar team. A role that provided the opportunity for him to develop his knowledge of ingredients and mixology skills (he practised constantly) so that he graduated to the position of fully-fledged bartender just one year later (a position he is immensely proud of). The Skinos Mediterranean Cocktail Challenge is a couples' competition, drawing on talent from the world over. In 2016, Constantinos came third, having incurred a time penalty! His return in 2017 saw him competing against teams from the USA, the UK and ten other countries. On this occasion, without any time penalties, he became champion alongside his teammate Alexis Argyrou.

WINNER OF SKINOS MEDITERRANEAN COCKTAIL CHALLENGE 2017

97

THYME DAIQUIRI
KAI WELLER

Kai says: I created the Thyme Daiquiri for the Havana Club competition. Having chosen to use Añejo Blanco, as I thought this best represents the essence of the rum, I invited my head chef to have a tasting with me to see what would work best (he wasn't hard to convince!). We decided the herbaceous notes of the young rum were complemented best by thyme, which also didn't overpower the delicate notes of the cocktail.

50ML HAVANA AÑEJO BLANCO RUM
6 SPRIGS OF THYME
25ML FRESH LIME JUICE
15ML GOMME SYRUP
15ML HOMEMADE THYME SYRUP*

METHOD: Add all the ingredients to a shaker with a scoop of ice and shake hard for 10 seconds (you want to release as much of the flavour from the thyme sprigs as possible). Double strain into a coupette glass and garnish with 2 thyme sprigs.

HOMEMADE THYME SYRUP*
Heat 500ml water with 500g sugar until the sugar has dissolved. Add 12 sprigs of thyme and simmer for 10 minutes. Strain and allow to cool.

———————

KAI WELLER began his bartending career at the Lonsdale in London's Notting Hill. His training lasted an amazing four years, which included a six-month stint with industry legend, Dick Bradsell. Kai explains, 'Dick was mainly teaching me to make lemonades, over and over again until I finally understood the importance of balance in a drink.' Kai then went on to join Dre Masso (another giant of the UK cocktail scene) at The Worldwide Cocktail Club where he spent the next 10 years travelling to more than 20 countries training the world's bartenders. Kai has advised on the opening of some great London bars including Bungalow 8 in St Martin's Lane and The Booking Office at St Pancras Renaissance Hotel, where he also worked for a while to train the opening team. In addition to his Havana Club victory, Kai also has a second place in the National Don Julio Cocktail Competition to his name.

WINNER OF UK HAVANA CLUB COCKTAIL COMPETITION 2005

TICKET TO THE AMERICAN DREAM
BORJA CORTINA

Borja says: *The inspiration for my cocktail was to create one to drink with a hamburger. I therefore decided to include various hamburger ingredients within the cocktail. I also drew inspiration from two icons of American life: Firstly, Bourbon, representing American lifestyle, and, secondly, as mentioned, hamburgers, in this case representing the American pace of life, the stresses, 1950s, Cadillac cars and rock 'n' roll. I considered how these icons are represented in American movies and so decided to create a serve inspired by the cinema – popcorn.*

60ML BULLEIT BOURBON WHISKEY
15ML CARAMELISED ONION SYRUP*
15ML FRESH LEMON JUICE
1 TBSP BARBECUE SAUCE
1 TBSP CHEDDAR CHEESE SAUCE

METHOD: Add all the ingredients to a shaker with a scoop of ice and shake very hard and fast. Strain the cocktail into a small bottle and place the bottle in a plastic popcorn box with a straw. Surround the bottle with crushed ice to keep cool, then lay some cling film over the ice. Now top up the box with salted popcorn. You can also serve alongside a hamburger!

CARAMELISED ONION SYRUP*
Gently sauté one large onion with some sugar (to taste) and a drop of olive oil. When nicely browned and soft, gather the onion mixture in a muslin cloth and squeeze out all the juice. Now mix the juice with 200ml water and 200g caster sugar. Stir until the sugar has completely dissolved and then refrigerate.

BORJA CORTINA began bartending at the age of 20, working in a family friend's café, where he learned to mix his first Gin Fizzes. By the year 2000, he had opened his own small bar, El Palacio, where he did everything from washing the dishes to waiting and, of course, bartending. By 2006 he had added a small brewery and by 2009 it had expanded to include a lounge area. During this period, Borja became a skilled mixologist, delivering courses and presentations at events like London Cocktail Week and in locations across Spain, such as Madrid, Barcelona and Ibiza. It was at this stage of his career that he began competing in competitions, which has led to him having a major presence and success in the largest national competitions – Diageo World Class and Bacardi Legacy. Borja's skills are in great demand and as a consequence he regularly works with the world's biggest drinks brands.

WINNER OF DIAGEO WORLD CLASS SPAIN 2015
194

THE WALDORF COCKTAIL

GIOVANNI BAVAJEE

Giovanni says: *I was inspired by the signature Waldorf salad and have translated this unique dish into an even more unique cocktail. I wanted guests at the Waldorf Hotel to indulge in the memorable taste of apple, walnuts, celery and grapes within a cocktail. My hope is that it becomes as well recognised as the Waldorf salad itself.*

35ML GIN
10ML APPLE LIQUEUR
20ML RAISIN PURÉE*
30ML CELERY SYRUP**
15ML CELERY PURÉE***
20ML FRESH LEMON JUICE

METHOD: Add all the ingredients to a shaker with a scoop of ice and shake for 30 seconds. Double strain into a cocktail glass filled with crushed ice. Garnish with 2 slices of green apple and a celery stick and add crushed walnuts to the top.

RAISIN PURÉE*
Put 5 tbsp raisins in a medium bowl. Add hot water to the top and leave them to soften. Once they are soft, strain the raisins and place in the blender with 60ml sugar syrup and 30ml water, then blend until you have a nice and soft purée.

CELERY SYRUP**
Boil 500g sugar, then add 5 sticks of celery and let them boil for 10 minutes until all the flavours come together. Allow to cool (this usually takes 30-45 minutes), then strain the syrup into a bottle.

CELERY PURÉE***
Place 4-6 celery sticks in a blender and add 120ml apple juice. Blend until it becomes a purée. It's very important to double strain it after this.

GIOVANNI BAVAJEE is unusual for a modern mixologist. In a world of bartenders plying their trade internationally for multiple companies and venues, subsequent to his early years Giovanni has spent the total of his high-level bartending career with the same hotel group in the same location: Ras al Khaimah in the UAE. Originally from Mauritius, Giovanni learnt his trade at a range of hotel bars before joining the Hilton group in 2009. In 2010 he made the move to the UAE and since then has ascended the bartending ladder rapidly, with his current position being food and beverage manager of the sensational Waldorf Astoria. Giovanni has won the Hilton Worldwide Best Mixologist award three years running, which is a unique achievement and underlines his cutting-edge creativity.

WINNER OF HILTON WORLDWIDE MASTERS, BEST MIXOLOGIST 2013

WHY THE SOUR FACE?!
ARIEL LEIZGOLD

Ariel says: The cocktail I have created is the simplest homage to one of the world's most famous drinks, the Whiskey Sour. At Bellboy our quest is to show our own view on the simplest things in life, in this case, a classic drink that takes on a local, redefined, comical stance. Making this Mediterranean version of the Whiskey Sour was a great ride and showcased in a very simple way our take on modern cocktail making.

50ML BOURBON INFUSED WITH ROASTED SESAME*
20ML FRESH LEMON JUICE
15ML SUGAR SYRUP
1 DROP ORANGE FLOWER WATER
2.5ML AMARO AVERNA LIQUEUR
5ML AMARO MONTENEGRO LIQUEUR

METHOD: Shake all the ingredients with a scoop of ice, then strain into a rocks glass (I used a 'sour-faced' mug). Garnish with Lemongrass Foam**.

BOURBON INFUSED WITH ROASTED SESAME*
Lightly toast a tablespoon of sesame seeds in a pan. Combine with 250ml bourbon in a container. Leave for 24 hours, then strain.

LEMONGRASS FOAM**
First brew 100ml lemongrass tea by infusing 1 chopped lemongrass stalk with 100ml hot water. Strain the liquid and add 1 tsp lecithin powder and stir. Now pump air into the mixture to create the foam. Ariel used an aquarium pump!

————

ARIEL LEIZGOLD can best be described as a cocktail 'magnate'. He is the founding owner of Monkey Business, a global bar consulting company, and has launched and owns many of Israel's most influential bars including 223, Duckface, Kalamata, Bellboy and Butler. He is also the brains behind The Locksmith which opened in Guangzhou, China in early 2017. He is the most decorated Israeli bartender in history, having won the national championship on nine occasions. Added to that are his two victories in the global finals of the Finlandia Vodka Cup (2006 and 2013), his third place in the very prestigious International Bartender's Association World Cocktail Competition, and of course his featured award-winning cocktail. Voted in 2011 to be included in Israel's 50 Most Influential Hospitality People list by *City Mouse* magazine, Ariel released his own bartender training book, *Zman Amiti* in 2012.

YELLOW CROCODILE
JONAS STERN

Jonas says: *The cocktail is inspired by Leonetto Cappiello's advertising for Fernet-Branca. The yellow crocodile alludes to the main ingredient of Fernet – crocus sativus or saffron – meaning 'yellow', and with its crocodile connotation, 'crocus', it was a smart advertisement. The powder sugar 'crusta' in my cocktail as well as the garnish of the zig-zag lemon peel refer to the crocodile's skin. To this day, Fernet controls 75 per cent of the world's saffron market. Hence saffron syrup is a vital ingredient in my cocktail.*

30ML FERNET-BRANCA
15ML GIN
15ML SAFFRON SYRUP*
10ML MINUS 8 ICE WINE VINEGAR**
10ML QUAGLIA CHINOTTO BITTER ORANGE LIQUEUR

METHOD: Add all the ingredients to a shaker with a scoop of ice. Shake and double strain into a flute glass encrusted with Saffron Powder Sugar***. Garnish with lemon peel with zig-zag cuts to the edges.

SAFFRON SYRUP*
In a pan, warm together 1kg sugar, 500ml water and 10g saffron. Strain the mixture and chill.

MINUS8** is available widely on trade but any other sweet vinegar will suffice

SAFFRON POWDER SUGAR***
Blend powdered (icing) sugar with saffron in a bar blender or food processor. Spray the glass with water using an atomiser, then sprinkle the sugar mixture until the glass is completely covered.

JONAS STERN is originally from Germany but has spent the majority of his bartending career working in London, with a short stint in Australia. Prior to becoming a bartender, Jonas had an internship at the world-renowned El Bulli restaurant as a commis chef. However, it was with mixology and bartending that Jonas discovered his true calling and since then he has tended bar at some of the finest hotels that London has to offer including the Corinthia, Claridges and the 5-star Connaught where he is currently the assistant bars manager. Jonas also spent a year and a half at Jason Atherton's Michelin-starred Pollen Street Social, where he was working at the time of his Fernet UK win. Jonas has featured in Skye Gyngell's book, *Spring*, and is also the winner of the Remy Centurion award.

WINNER OF FERNET-BRANCA UK COCKTAIL COMPETITION 2016

Dale says: *In this particular case I started the dinner at the bar with the writer and the photographer Nancy Newman. The cocktail was the Negroni. The Negroni and Campari did not enjoy the popularity they do today and they both found the drink unpleasantly bitter.*

It was shaping up to be a PR nightmare for the sponsor Bacardi (I was using their Bombay Gin and their Martini & Rossi Sweet Vermouth), so I collected their drinks and added Cointreau and orange juice to the sweet vermouth, gin and Campari and repackaged the drink as a fancy cocktail ... they were very happy with the result. So in essence my winning drink The Old Flame (double meaning to include the famed orange zest garnish) was a desperate attempt to pull a victory out of the jaws of defeat!

Well it worked and they decided that the reworked drink (I called it the Fancy Nancy after the photographer) was their favourite of all the drinks that evening. Down the road my relationship with the Bacardi brand portfolio led to another opportunity. The international brand manager contacted me and suggested that after 40 years of the Bacardi Martini Grand Prix drinks contest, an American had never competed ... I was invited to compete that year, 2001.

The drink I chose was the accidental concoction from that dinner. I changed the name to The Old Flame a title with wonderful repercussions for lots of people and one that also gave me the opportunity to wow the judges with my flaming orange peel.

I won best fancy cocktail that year ... the first American to win anything in the competition!

INDEX

PHOTO CREDITS
Special thanks to Tom Foot for all his help in taking the many cocktail photographs featured throughout this book that were not otherwise supplied.

————————

© Eugene Lee: page xii
© John Mailley: pages 3, 203
© Tom Foot: pages 4, 15, 19, 20, 27, 28, 32, 36, 51, 56, 72, 76, 80, 84, 88, 92, 103, 104, 111, 112, 115, 127, 136, 144, 151, 175, 176, 188, 192
© Rian Asiddao: page 7
© Manolis Lykiardopoulos: page 8
© Patrón: pages 11, 35, 59, 67, 120, 184
© Grace Tsai: page 12
© Anya Montague: page 16
© Engin Yildiz: page 23
© Valentino Longo: page 24
© Caleb Krivoshei: page 31
© Pieter D'Hoop: page 39
© Wang Jiling Tyler: page 40
© Lora Hoare: page 43
© Antonio Neranjo Nevares: page 44
© Sondre Innvær: page 47
© Jack Hawkins: page 48
© Francesco Cione: page 52
© Giacomo Vezzo: page 55
© Jennifer Le Nechet: page 60
© Maria Diego Alvarez: pages 63, 191
© Michael Norat: page 64
© Nick Wu: page 68
© Henry Siktimu: page 71
© Dale DeGroff: page 75
© PhotoOle: page 79
© Jamie Stephenson Photography: page 83
© Kneale Brown: page 87
© Jim Gates, Blue Dot Studios Grand Cayman: page 91
© Tony Pereyra: page 95
© Diageo: page 96

© Tyrone Holguin: page 99
© Piotr Jakubina: page 100
© Jean van Luelik: page 107
© Akkapat Inthuprapa: pages ii, 108
© João Rodrigues: page 116
© Amir Yakoby, Akkerman LTD: page 119
© Kennedy Nascimento: page 123
© Kentaro Satoh: page 124
© Bacardi: page 128
© Jacko Chang: page 131
© Alexander Banck-Petersen, Cocktails of Copenhagen: page 132
© PR Jasper Johns: page 135
© Antonio Calanni: page 139
© Ayip Dzuhri: page 140
© Ryu Fuji: page 143
© Shawn Chong: page 147
© Adam Schell: page 148
© Ryan Wainwright: page 152
© Valter Fabiano, Balthazar Media: page 155
© Regeri Zoo: page 156
© BLCC Global: page 159
© Karl Petersson: page 160
© Blair Frodelius: page 163
© Tore Berger: page 164
© Peter Gózon: page 167
© Ron's Cocktail Service: page 168
© David Hartung: page 171
© Felix Patrisius Sani: page 172
© Steve Leong: page 179
© Pailin Sajjanit: page 180
© Laura Duca: page 183
© Soufiane El Alaoui: page 187
© Hector Torra: page 195
© Giovanni Bavajee: page 196
© Studio Moloko and Roshiano: page 199
© Jonas Stern: page 200